# TIGER TRACKS

# TIGER TRACKS

## Three Days on the Eastern Front

### WOLFGANG FAUST

Translated from the memoir
'Panzerdammerung'
('Panzer Twilight')

ISBN: 1539588114
ISBN-13: 9781539588115

# ORIGINAL INTRODUCTION FROM THE AUTHOR

Only those who experienced our war in the East can truly picture its scale and ferocity. There are many of us who were there; I believe that of the 20 million men who served under German arms from 1939 to 1945, 17 million served exclusively on the Russian front. Yet, the survivors are less than that number, and our experience is not readily discussed in public today.

For this reason, I have written this book, which for me encapsulates the spirit of that war, with its slaughter, chaos, universal destruction and its strange bravery on all sides. I have drawn on what I experienced as a Tiger panzer crew man; nothing that I have set down here is exaggerated or confected.

Some press critics have already said that this book is 'needlessly controversial,' 'too provocative' or even 'too violent,' comments which seem incredible when applied to a book about the East. I note that these criticisms come chiefly from civilian reviewers who were not present at the front. From those who were there in the panzers, in the dust, snow and mud, I have received confirmation that the book is true to the life that we led and the way that we gave battle. Such confirmation is all that I sought.

Wolfgang Faust

*Köln am Rhein*
*July 1948*

# TIGER TRACKS

*Western Russia, October 1943*

**B**etween the mud and the snow, Russia gave us ice. And in the ice, my God, that Tiger was a heavy lump of iron to drive. Sixty tonnes of the Reich's finest metal, fitted with the widest tracks ever designed – but still, in that frozen Russia, the *verdamm* beast would slither and claw its way around, with me riding its gears like a boy riding a dragon.

It was bad enough in the assembly area that morning, as our company of twenty Tiger I panzers came in from their conceal-ment points and began to form up before dawn, with their exhausts sparking flames and their great dish wheels throwing out icicles one metre long. But when we heard the order '*Panzer Marsch!*' and we surged out to form up into our arrowhead, with our lead tank at the tip of the arrow, and the others in a flying v-shape behind him, our twenty 88mm guns pointing at the heart of the Red zone – that was when it got tough for this humble panzer driver.

We were advancing east across three kilometres of steppe, right into the Ivan army's flank, heading for a line of Red bunkers on higher ground that we had to destroy. Three kilometres of freezing tundra, filled with bomb craters, other destroyed tanks and the little tricks that the Reds liked to play on us German boys.

If our Tiger slid through the mist into one of those craters, with deep water under the crust of ice, then our panzer would become a U-boat. If our vehicle collided with one of the wrecked T34s still smouldering from the previous day's combat, then we might detonate their ammunition or damage our precious track links. And if we ran into one of Ivan's special traps – the anti-tank ditch concealed with straw, or the flamethrower that ignited when a panzer rolled over a cable – then we'd breathe our last gulp of Russian air, if we were lucky. The less fortunate might survive, and take the prison wagon to Siberia.

Peering through my armoured vision slit at the steppe out in front, and following my commander's instructions from up in the turret cupola, I dreaded any of these things happening to our Tiger; despite our armour plate, I had the sweating hands and dry throat that always came from facing the big Red war machine.

In the east, the winter sun began to rise like a piece of hot iron, but it gave no warmth to the landscape, which stayed shrouded in low mist and drifts of ice. Overhead, three of our Focke-Wulf fighters streaked forward, trailing vapour, and then a slow, lumbering flight of six Stukas heading out to soften up those Ivan bunkers for our Tigers to maul.

Inside our panzer, it was humid now, as the groaning transmission became hot and warmed the sealed-in air. Condensation collected on my dials, scalding oil from the transmission spat on my face, the reek of carbon monoxide made my head throb, and I almost envied our commander up in the turret, still with his head up in the morning air – despite the risk he ran of losing that clever brain to a shell or a sniper.

'What a stench!' the gruff voice next to me muttered. 'If they could bottle this cologne for me to wear, I won't be troubled by so many blondes on my next leave in Hamburg.'

Our radio operator and hull machine-gunner, Kurt, was the ugliest bastard in the Heavy Panzer Battalion – and my best comrade. I didn't have to look at him over the shuddering transmission housing to know he was sighting down the eyepiece of his MG34, and monitoring the signals from our other panzers with his great, deformed ears in his headphones.

3

In front of us, the line of Tigers on our side of the surging arrowhead sprayed up plumes of mud and ice into the reddening sky, maintaining a steady 20kph that allowed us to stay in formation and make good time across the no-man's steppe.

The ground ahead was barren, with just the hulk of another burned-out T34 between us and the ridge in the distance where the target bunkers were sited. Up there, I could see the crooked, black shapes of the Stukas peeling and diving out of the dawn sky, diving almost vertically – and as I watched, great spouts of debris shot up as their bombs exploded on the Ivan forts.

I wiped my sweating forehead on my sleeve, and glanced around momentarily at the base of the turret cage. I saw three pairs of feet in there: the scuffed lace-up boots of our 88mm gunner and our loader – and the polished jackboots of Oberleutnant Helmann, our vehicle commander. The shine on those boots was legendary, like Helmann's coolness in action, his taste for cognac and his hatred of the Reds. I glanced back at my vision slit, and made a slight change to the differential, steering us around the wrecked T34. The Ivan tank was a blackened hulk, surrounded by debris, with its tracks hanging off and its gun pointing down.

I blinked as I looked at that T34. It was perhaps 200 metres away, outlined against the skyline, and through the mist on my vision block I thought I saw the *verdamm* thing moving its gun.

'What the *scheisse?*' Kurt grunted beside me. 'That Ivan is moving.'

I wasn't sure what I was seeing. This smashed, burned tank, with its tracks lying in spools on the steppe around it, was elevating its 76mm gun, and its turret was traversing onto us. What the hell was going on here?

'Fire on the Red!' Helmann shouted over the headphones – the order was to our gunner, who lived with his face glued to the eye-piece of the gun sight. 'Fire on him!'

I heard our turret traverse with its drive motor, as our gunner calibrated on the T34, which now had its barrel pointed at our whole flank of ten panzers, aiming at hull sides where our armour was comparatively thinner. Our other Tigers were traversing onto him too – all the crews had observed that this hulk was apparently coming to life.

That T34 got off one single shot before he was blown to pieces.

His muzzle flashed and spat fire – and at the same moment, he was hit by half a dozen armour-piercing shells from the Tiger muzzle brakes that spat, smoked and recoiled in unison at the intruder.

In our turret, the huge gun barked, and the shell case sprang out with a clang.

Two things happened straight away.

First, the T34 disintegrated as the broadside of 88mm shells smashed into its armour at zero range. The turret split open, and for a moment I saw a man in there – a single gunner – twisting as his carapace was blown apart. Then he too disappeared as the hull below him was demolished, with the deck separating from the walls and the sloped glacis plate breaking into pieces that span away in the air like bits of a tin can. His ammunition in there exploded, and the mangled turret ring gave out a blast of sparks and flames that rose high above our column.

A beacon of success – but at the same time, I saw that the Tiger at the very tip of our spearhead, our leading panzer, was shuddering and throwing out metal treads from its tracks. Suddenly, its whole track on the right side came flying out backwards, thrashing in the wake of the rear idler wheel like a horse-whip. Track links broke off and hit the following panzers; then the damaged Tiger slowed down in a spray of mud, and juddered to a halt.

'That Red bastard hit the Boss,' Helmann said coolly over the headphones. 'The Boss is stranded here now, the poor soul.'

'Shall I halt, sir?' I asked over the intercom.

'No panzer can halt,' Helmann replied. 'These are our orders.'

The Boss was our commander – our Hauptmann – who had led the unit since the glory days of Barbarossa. Now Helmann, as his second-in-command, would automatically take over the leader's role.

Kurt winked at me over the bulkhead separating us. To lead the Heavy Panzer Unit into an attack – that was always Helmann's wish – and now he had it.

The Boss's damaged panzer remained stranded, while the following Tigers moved around it without slowing or losing formation. Briefly, I saw the immobilised Tiger as we went past it, with its track blown off by that single shell from the T34 before the Russian was destroyed. The static Tiger's crew were starting to clamber from their hatches to assess the damage – but we could all see that the track was smashed, and the vehicle would be unable to move without a recovery panzer to bring a whole new length of track links.

'Maybe that's a bad omen,' Kurt muttered beside me, changing his mood. 'How did that wrecked Ivan manage to take a shot?'

'Such is the Red Army,' Helmann said without emotion, speaking from the turret through our headphones. 'They find a gunner who's made some mistake, they tell him his family will go to Siberia unless he dies a hero's death, and they put him in a wrecked tank that still has a half-way working gun. They tow it out here at night and dump it, with him inside and a few shells.'

'That's how it works, is it?' Kurt said into the intercom. 'If I was him, I'd jump out and hand myself over to good German hospitality.'

'Ah, but they put a padlock on the hatches,' Helmann said. 'And they tell him to think of his lovely wife who won't enjoy the Arctic Circle. Now enough of talking, and let's watch for any more of these Red games. We are close to the target here.'

'The Boss, sir –' I said.

'He'll be ok, Faust. Keep driving.'

I had no time to reflect on what chance our stranded Boss and his crew had of surviving in the steppe. We all knew that the disputed tundra held Red infantry fighters hidden in lairs, who would begin to emerge and prowl around any immobilised panzer. But at that point, we had our own battle to fight.

Ahead of us, the diving Stukas had left vertical trails in the freezing air that still remained sharp, like twists of steel wire against the dawn. They pointed downward to the fires and clouds of dust where their bombs had struck, pulverising the Red bunkers and block-houses that we were now to attack, to crush and overrun. We knew, though, that the Reds were at their most vicious when they'd taken a beating – like surly Red dogs, Helmann often said.

We were about 1500 metres from the enemy bunkers, close enough to see the smoke drifting from the Stuka bomb craters. I was feeling jumpy, as I so often did in action, as each minute seemed to stretch out interminably, every second full of the threat of a mine under the tracks, or a heavy-calibre PAK round smashing through the bulkhead beside my head. The stench of the Tiger's compart-ment was overlaid with the bitter scent of the 88mm blast. I wished the waiting was over, and we could start firing, or manoeuvring, or anything other than this slow, onward advance under the eyes of the watching Reds.

The waiting ended when the smoke around the bunkers parted – and a stream of T34 tanks came pouring out to face us.

I laughed with a weird relief – and beside me, big, ugly Kurt did the same, hunched over his MG34 stock, moving the ball-mount left and right across the ground ahead. Through my headphones, I heard the rapid discussion between Helmann and our gunner, and I heard the loader grunting as he seized another round of armour-piercing in readiness. Then the orders came fast and furious, as the Russian tanks charged towards us across the wretched steppe of their homeland.

Even through the specks of mud on my vision block, I could see that these were the upgraded type of T34s, with enlarged turrets and the long 85mm gun they carried to deal with us dashing lads in our Tigers. Their hulls were thinner than ours, though, and against our high-velocity 88mm warheads, any kind of strike from us was a danger to them. Their only hope was to get close enough to make their guns count – and this was their tactic, setting their thicker front plates towards us and accelerating, with their bulbous turret fronts leaning forwards…

'Like dogs,' Helmann muttered, using his favourite metaphor. 'Like a pack of dogs.'

His voice was drowned out as our 88mm fired – and the Tiger flattened down in its motion as the breech recoiled. Smoke from the muzzle breech clouded my vision momentarily, and when that cleared I saw our Tigers spreading out from their arrowhead, moving into a broad arc that stretched for a kilometre left and right across the plain. I moved our Tiger into the line, being roughly in the centre, and aimed our panzer for the Russian bunker line that we had to smash through. I saw one of these T34s, barely a kilometre away now, explode on first contact with our ordinance – the turret lifting up into the air and spinning over repeatedly, scattering the burning remains of the gun crew behind it. The hull itself flashed and blew up in a blaze of fuel.

I focussed on a little pack of three Red tanks that was advancing in our direction, with mud flying around them as they charged towards the centre of our line.

'Slow down,' Helmann told me. 'Steady the gun on this uneven ground, man.'

I went down to 10 kph, so the rolling terrain would have less effect on the accuracy of the gun. The split second between our gunner pulling his trigger and the shell leaving the muzzle was now made more stable, but of course we were a slower, easier target. We had to trust in the 10cm of steel on our front hull, and the 12cm on our turret. The Tigers beside us slowed similarly, and together we in the centre of the line fired repeatedly on the advancing Russian armour. That pack of three T34s took the brunt of our guns immediately, as lines of our bright red tracer shot towards them

I saw one of the Red machines take a hit on his front plate, which made the whole tank bounce and recoil, as a spray of metal pieces erupted from his armour. Another round hit him in the gun mantle, and the turret jerked to one side at the blow, but the 88mm round deflected off and went spinning wildly across the steppe. A third round pierced him between the turret and hull – and the whole gun mantle exploded off, leaving a gaping hole which gushed with sparks.

Defenceless, the tank tried to turn to flee – but as its panicking driver slewed to one side, he presented his thinner hull flank, and paid the price for his mistake as another line of tracer penetrated the crew compartment there. I saw the wrecked turret spurt a plume of flames from the broken mantle and the turret hatch, and the whole vehicle span around on its axis, out of control, pouring with fire.

I did not spare any emotion for the burning crew boys; my simple mind, trained in the backstreets of Munich to watch for danger, turned attention to the other two T34s, who were now halted in a spray of mud some 500 metres from me. Their muzzles flashed, and I saw green tracer race towards us. There was a crash from in front of me, and the electric light over my head exploded, showering me with fragments. My transmission raced for a moment, slipping the gears, and then I got the beast under control and prevented it sliding sideways on to the enemy. We were hit on the front plate beside my head, between Kurt and me, but the great Tiger kept on rolling slowly forward, and our 88mm kept booming out from the turret behind me.

Through the mist of blast gas, oil fumes and exhaust in our hull, I saw in my vision slit the tank that had just fired being hit in the right hand track, which flew up into the air, dragging with it the steel drive wheel. Crippled, it tried to reverse – but it simply dug a grave for itself with its running track, which raced around and sank deep into the mud. Its gun kept on firing, and the Tiger beside us was hit on the turret in a shower of sparks, until one of our shells punched into the T34's bow, close to its smashed front wheels, and split open the armour plate.

We advanced as that tank began to burn, and its crew began to emerge from the hatches to escape the flames. Next to me, the compartment echoed as Kurt loosed off two seconds from his gimbal-mounted MG34, catching the Russians as they clambered out onto the hull and turret. He cut them down, then ceased fire, breathing hard and cursing to himself.

I never knew if he liked the killing, or if he hated it.

The third of these T34s that we were facing in our section now began to reverse, firing wildly as it went back, throwing up a curtain of black mud, ice and debris from its wide tracks. Indeed, as I glanced left and right along our line, I could just make out that the T34s were generally retreating from us, although one of our Tigers had been set on fire and was burning with a crimson glow around its engine deck. I saw the shapes of maybe five of the Russian tanks, burning or pouring smoke, one with its turret shot away and another lying on its side with its tracks still turning slowly in the air.

I began to think that success was upon us.

Ahead, behind the retreating T34s, pursued as they were by our angry tracer rounds, the bunker line stood smashed and burning against the ridge of higher ground that it was supposed to defend.

Ahead of me, I suddenly saw the retreating T34 grind to a halt and face us defiantly, its muzzle shooting three rounds in rapid succession along our line. There was a colossal crash as we were hit in the turret, causing a shrieked curse from our loader and a grim chuckle from Helmann. In response, our cool gunner put an 88mm shell straight into the halted tank's frontal plate; the round blew off the driver's vision block armour in a starburst of debris – but still the T34 remained defiant.

'Ah, I see, I see why,' Helmann muttered, and I heard his polished boots click behind me on the floor of the turret cage as he moved around, checking the view from the radial periscopes in his cupola. 'I see. There's an anti-tank ditch behind that Ivan tank. It's deep, too. It goes all along our line. *Verdamm!*'

I brought the Tiger to a halt, and along our row of panzers, the other Tigers stopped or slowed as their commanders too realised the danger.

From my hull position, I couldn't see the ditch – I could only see the T34, still firing at us – but if it was like the other Ivan ditches, it was four metres deep and the same wide, just enough to trap a magnificent Tiger and its handsome German crew by toppling it nose-down into the Russian depths. Sometimes these ditches contained mines or aircraft bombs which were rigged to explode when a panzer fell in; others were filled with pools of gasoline which were primed to detonate, incinerating the trapped vehicle.

I had seen some of these ditches that had been dug by German prisoners, with the bodies of our men still strewn in the pit, dead where they laboured and dug; and, of course, our own anti-tank ditches were full of dead Soviet prisoners who were worked to death likewise. This was Russia.

Helmann swore long and hard at this obstruction, his boot soles scraping around behind me as he studied the situation. Then his cursing turned to a crescendo, and he yelled,

'Hull gunner! Where are your eyes, man? The Reds are in front of you.'

In justice to Kurt, I could not see the problem either. Being low down and right at the front, our vision apertures were coated with mud and ice, and the sighting glass on the bow MG34 was notoriously prone to become obscured. But then Kurt grunted viciously, hunched over and began firing his MG34 in long bursts, moving his shoulders around frantically as he aimed at the targets he saw.

In front of my block, I suddenly witnessed a lone Red soldier, in a fur cap and quilted jacket, appear from a hole in the ground barely twenty metres away, throwing back a straw cover and vaulting out onto the steppe – followed by another Ivan doing the same. In moments, the ground in front of us was dotted with these brown scarecrows, all of them dodging and weaving between our MG tracer as they battled to get close to our panzers.

I feared these devils more than I feared a T34.

These Red Army anti-tank infantry lived and breathed for killing Tigers; they fought with hand-mines, satchel bombs and even Molotov bottles thrown onto the fan grilles of our engine decks. It took just one of them to get close, to throw his bomb – and our engine would suck in fire or fragments through the rear grilles, setting off our oil and gasoline and bringing our Wehrmacht careers to a fiery conclusion.

Kurt was doing what he could, hosing down the ground with MG fire, giving the Reds no chance to approach, and the Tiger on our left was blasting away, lowering its main gun too so that the co-axial MG could aim at the ground, and traversing left and right to keep up a murderous semi-circle of bullets. All the time, though, that T34 behind the emerging infantry was shooting at us, and I felt the Tiger rock as we took hit after hit on our turret and bow plate.

One of the T34's shells actually saved our necks: it deflected off our bow, and flew straight back in a burst of metal scabs. The spinning warhead tore into a Russian soldier as he was running towards us, carrying a mine, crouched down low. The shell decapitated him and then hit the belly of the man behind him. Both bodies kept running towards us for a moment, until they slumped down. They exploded as their mines detonated, sending their severed limbs flailing across the ground.

Our gunner silenced that *verdamm* Ivan tank with two shots, one through the driver's visor, and another that tore off its left track and wheels, sending bits of the drive wheel into the air for hundreds of metres. That tank began to smoulder, the barrel slumped, and our gunner immediately lowered our main gun and began spraying MG onto the infantry, as our comrade panzer beside us was doing.

Beside me, my big, ugly Kurt fired MG until his ammunition cylinder gave out, and then he began to change it with a suitable muttered commentary, referring to the generally inefficient designs of the Spandau gunsmiths in terms of magazine capacity – and also to the sexual tastes of their mothers. In the pause, the Red infantry surged forward from the right hand side, these mud-covered creatures that I could just see in the corner of my glass block, grinning and shouting with their wild eyes fixed on our superb panzer. It was a desperate moment, and I took desperate measures to protect us.

Normally, a panzer did not like to approach enemy foot soldiers armed with hand-bombs; the risks were too high, and our engine grilles were too vulnerable. But now I got close to these Red bastards, close enough to give them a view of our dish wheels and steel track links working in unison. With a shout of encouragement from

Helmann, I threw the Tiger into gear; my right hand forward and my left hand pulling back on the differential wheel, I span its 60 tonnes around on its axis, so that the churning wheels and tracks rotated in a circle towards the onrushing Red troops.

I didn't even feel their bodies being crushed and chewed by the tracks – there wasn't even a jolt as we ran them down in clusters. Human flesh was too soft to withstand these forces, too frail to even register on my dials. I saw three of the Ivans try to run, in front of my vision slit, until the square hull front covered them up and only a dismembered leg in its felt boot tumbled up onto our glacis. I span and crushed the enemies down, with Kurt beside me blasting now on his MG34 at any who jumped clear – and together, we defended that corner of Russia on behalf of the Reich.

I brought the panzer to a halt, facing the ditch, at an angle that gave me a good view of our comrade Tiger on the left. He was surrounded by dead and crushed Red infantry also, and he began to elevate his gun to take aim again at the Russian bunkers. I saw one of the dead Russians, apparently a blood-covered body, suddenly shake, crawl to his knees – and throw a bomb onto our fellow panzer.

Kurt shot him down with his MG, and for safety he machine-gunned the other bodies lying nearby – but that one small Russian bomb did its terrible work. It landed on our fellow Tiger's back decking, where the engine fans spin under their armoured grilles, and I saw a flash of orange flame as its charge ignited. A simple Molotov – just a glass bottle of cheap kerosene and a percussion fuse, but enough to send a litre of burning liquid down into the Tiger's mighty Maybach engine.

Helmann cursed, and I heard him kick at the turret cage with his polished boots, but his anger could do nothing against the flames that were rising from the Tiger on our left. A spiral of flame shot up out of that Tiger's engine, accompanied by debris from the engine – and one of the grilles lifted off and span into the air. I saw the round hatch in the rear of the turret open, and the loader leaned out with an extinguisher, but the device spluttered and died in his hands. He threw it away, and the Tiger's other hatches opened as the crew began to evacuate before their fuel exploded.

Of the five men who exited, four were immediately cut down by Red small arms fire. The fifth fell onto the burning grilles, and lay there thrashing in the flames as the gasoline took hold below him.

I looked to see where those murderous bullets came from. I saw, on the T34 that was knocked out on the very edge of the anti-tank ditch, one of the Russian tank crew, still in his ribbed helmet, crouching behind the turret with its slumped gun barrel, aiming a machine pistol over the turret roof. Even out of the tank, these Red crews were determined to frustrate us and to cut us down. Kurt sprayed the man with MG34, and the fellow tumbled off his tank, his MP still firing into the air.

Suddenly, light and fresh air flooded down into our compartment, and I knew that Helmann had slid open his cupola hatch in the turret.

'Take us close to the burning Tiger,' he ordered me, and without asking why, I drove us the twenty metres over to the blazing vehicle, with its dead crew sprawled on its hull. Not all were dead, though – the man who had fallen onto the engine deck was still alive, flailing and twisting in the flames that slowly engulfed him from the burning Maybach engine under the grilles. When I halted our panzer, I heard two shots from our cupola – and the burning man ceased his tormented movements, and lay still in the flames.

That was a mercy.

I shook my head, and waited for Helmann's orders. I could hear him rotating in the cupola, looking for some way over the anti-tank ditch. The other Tigers were poised all along our line, expectant, static targets that needed to be moving forward, not sitting still on the open steppe. It was down to us to lead the way across here, and spearhead the victory that was so close.

'There is a way across,' Helmann said. 'There is a causeway that the T34s must have used. Advance to the edge, driver, and you will see.'

I span the panzer and drove up to the edge of the ditch. Yes, there was a narrow causeway over the anti-tank ditch; an earth ridge, barely wide enough for a Tiger to pass, but it looked solid, and capable of taking our weight. After all, it had just taken the weight of a dozen T34s that came charging out to meet us – T34s which now lay burning in our wake. This might enable us to cross over to our final objective of the bunker line itself.

'I'll drive over it, then, sir,' I said to Helmann on the intercom.

'Ja,' Kurt mimicked me. 'We'll be in Moscow for schnapps time.'

'No.' Helmann snapped. 'It will be mined for sure, or there will be a bomb concealed. One of those Reds will be hidden here, waiting to blow it as soon as a panzer advances.'

'Then what?' I mouthed to Kurt.

He shrugged.

'Depress the gun elevation,' Helmann said to our gunner. 'Shoot into the causeway, use high-explosive.'

'Shoot the causeway, Herr Ober?' the gunner repeated.

'You heard me.'

The gun system whined as the long 88mm declined to below horizontal, its massive barrel now visible in front of me. A moment later the gun barked. The smoke from the muzzle brake spiralled around and clouded my view, but a second later I saw the entire causeway explode.

My God, the blast.

That wasn't just an 88mm high-explosive round – that was a concealed munition, hidden somewhere inside the earth bridge, and detonated by our shell. The entire causeway lifted into the air, and big pieces of rock and stone went spinning away, left and right, for hundreds of metres. Our whole Tiger shook in the blast wave. Chunks of debris rained down on us, clanging on the steel roof, and pulverising the massed Russian bodies around us even further. A huge clod of earth splattered onto my vision port, obscuring my view completely.

'That has proved my point,' Helmann commented. 'I'd say that was a crate of howitzer shells, primed and waiting to go up.'

'I'm blind, sir,' I said.

'You, or the panzer?'

'The vision block, sir. It's covered in earth.'

'Get out and clean it, man. Be quick. And take a look at the ditch while you're there, Faust – can we cross it?'

I knew better than to query an order from Helmann – above all, with our massed column of angry Tigers behind us, itching to get moving over the obstacle. I opened the hatch above me, and clambered out onto the hull top. Cold air and the smell of explosive hit me immediately, as I leaned forward and pushed the earth away from the glass vision block under its steel eyelid.

I looked around. The sight was astonishing.

There were mangled Russian bodies everywhere. The causeway was utterly demolished, being now just a pile of rubble and earth inside the ditch, which was far too deep for us to drive across. Beyond it, the shattered bunkers lay drifting with smoke from the Stuka bombs, strangely inactive in the mist still clinging to the ground.

I climbed back inside the panzer and slammed the hatch.

'Well?' Helmann demanded. 'Can we cross over?'

'It's too deep now, sir. We'll need a bridging unit, or we need construction troops to fill it in.'

'No, we must cross. We must cross now. The Boss is gone, and we are the leading panzer.'

'We'll get stuck, sir.'

'Use that T34,' Helmann ordered. 'The one on the edge of the ditch. Make use of him.' I felt Helmann's boot give me a sharp kick between the shoulder blades as I hesitated. He liked to hang down by his arms from the turret and kick me or Kurt in this manner, if he thought we were being slow. 'Do it, Faust. Ram that T34 into the ditch.'

I could see what he meant us to do, but the risk was enormous.

The wrecked T34 that had sought to defy us on the edge of the ditch, whose crew man had shot our people as their Tiger burned – that tank was still in place, its tracks blown off by our shooting and by the blast from the causeway bomb, but still a big lump of Soviet iron that could fill a hole in the ground. I manoeuvred our Tiger up to its shattered hull, aware that all the Tiger crews behind me were watching my performance – and those handsome boys would not forgive a mistake. I put my glacis plate up to the sloped front of the T34, and felt the resistance as our 600 horse power pushed on the Russian's static weight in the mud. I cursed, engaged lowest gear, and pushed again.

My whole vision block was filled with the front plate of the T34, with its smashed driver's port and wrecked front drive wheels. The Russian machine began to slide back in the mud, slowly but clearly, a metre at a time, towards the ditch. I saw the hatch on the front deck of the T34 open; a pale, confused face appeared in the gap, covered in blood. This Russian crewman stared at me through my glass block, blinking as he apparently regained consciousness, unable to believe what he was witnessing.

I kept pushing his tank back with our nose, with this man looking me in the eyes from barely four metres distance. He seemed to realise where he was and what was happening, because he began to struggle, trying to pull himself out of the hatch as his tank started to tip back into the ditch behind. The Russian lad mouthed a few words, then opened his mouth and screamed as the whole T34 slid down, tail first, into the ditch, and disappeared from view as it came to rest upside down, on the piles of rubble in the pit.

'Good,' Helmann observed – the highest compliment he ever awarded. 'The Red is lying crosswise in the ditch, filling it for us. Drive over him, Faust.'

'Yes, sir.'

Beside me, Kurt seized hold of the hand-grabs, knowing from experience what crossing a filled-in ditch was like. Using the steering control, though, I had nothing else to cling on to; as I took the Tiger forward, our great armoured nose tipped down and crashed into the pit. I saw the T34's belly plate below us on the remains of the causeway, filling up the lower three metres of the hole, and in a moment our tracks crashed onto his deck.

I lost a tooth as the impact shook my skull, and I felt the T34 sink as our weight hit him, but our momentum was such that, with a blast of throttle that had the transmission spitting oil at me, our tracks got traction and our front hull clawed up and over the opposite bank of the ditch. Spitting blood and tooth fragments, I brought our Tiger thumping down onto the bunker side, the torsion bar suspension rods howling in protest – although I knew that they secretly enjoyed a little rough treatment.

'Good,' Helmann said again.

'*Gut!*' Kurt muttered to me. 'You'll be Reich Inspector of Panzer Forces at this rate.'

'The Tigers are crossing behind us,' Helmann said proudly. From his cupola, he had all-round vision, whereas I could only see in front of me. 'Two panzers are across behind us, and now three.' He chuckled his weird little laugh. 'Now keep moving, driver, don't remain a static target. Let's clear out these rats nests, and then the place is ours.'

I drove over to the wreckage of the nearest bunker. This was a wide, squat concrete box with slit embrasures, in which the barrels of wrecked PAK guns pointed at crazy angles, crushed by the blown-in roof. As we approached, I saw flashes from inside, and I heard the faint jangle of small arms fire hitting our armour plate. One bullet clipped the edge of my vision block, and cracked it with a long split. Our gunner immediately lowered the 88mm, and fired three rounds of high-explosive into the remains of the bunker's apertures. The bunker walls collapsed, and the structure slumped into dust, together with whoever was determined to hold out inside of there for his mother Russia.

Out from the back end of the wreckage, a handful of ragged individuals emerged, their quilted jackets thick with soot and smoking from the blast. They raised their hands and swayed on their feet, staring up at us. Kurt shot them down with one second from his MG, and then muttered to himself as he changed his magazines again. The Russians lay in front of us on the ice, breathing their last.

'Now we spread out and secure the zone for our Panzergrenadiers,' Helmann said, and he began talking on the intercom to other tank commanders, with Kurt, as the radio operator, patching him through to them with his valve set.

———

Five minutes later, we seemed to be in complete control. Helmann, as acting commander of our unit, was trying to contact our Divisional command by radio to inform them of our success. This was an uncertain process, though, as our radio set was not the Boss's high-capacity unit; ours was designed only for contact between tanks, not over long distances. While that went on, I was given permission to exit the panzer and check the running gear and wheels for damage.

I climbed up onto the hull, and took in the scene of our victory. All along the sloping ground beyond the bunkers, our Tigers were climbing to the ridge at the top, taking up their commanding fire position that would guard the main thrust of our *Kampfgruppe* battle group through the centre of the Soviet lines, ten kilometres to the south.

That was the plan, and the plan was working so far.

I checked our track links and dish wheels, finding them in good order, although the links would need tightening and the rear idler wheels were bleeding lubricant. The tracks were coated in bits of human debris from our clash with the Red infantry before the ditch – hair, boots, fingers and long, bloody shreds of flesh. Cleaning this stuff out was a miserable job that we usually allocated to prisoners.

Indeed, huddled against a bunker nearby was a sad group of ten live Russians whose surrender we had accepted, as they appeared to be part of a radio operating team. A radio team was a good catch, and they might hold useful intelligence; but, like all prisoners, they would be put to work cleaning our track links and doing whatever lifting and carrying we needed, before they were taken away for processing.

One of these prisoners in particular attracted our men's attention. She was a young woman, apparently some kind of junior radio officer, that we wanted to prioritise for interrogation because of her rank and her potential knowledge. She stood there scowling, with her arms folded across the front of her male uniform, her hair in coppery coils around her neck.

Behind us, the anti-tank ditch was properly bridged now: a *Sturmpioner* engineers unit had come up with a steel gantry bridge on a Panzer IV chassis, and slung it across the chasm, away from the wrecked causeway and the crushed T34 that we had used as an emergency filler. Our supporting Panzergrenadier infantry had caught up with us, and were crossing the steel bridge in their Hanomag half-tracked vehicles, then fanning out across the land behind the Tigers, so that we were a true little occupying army up here on the Russian heights.

Some of the Hanomag troops yelled at me as their half-track paused nearby.

'Who dumped the Ivan in the ditch, Faust?'

'I did it myself.'

'*Scheisse!* You learned a lot when your daddy was driving that tram, didn't you?'

I gave them a cheerful underarm salute, and they returned it as their vehicle drove on up the ridge. But yes, I thought, looking at a mangled Russian belt buckle wedged in my front drive wheel. I learned a lot from my daddy driving that tram, when I was sitting on his knee and hearing stories of the first war –

'Wake up, man!' Helmann's voice was loud in my ear. 'You drove well today. Don't go to sleep on me now.'

'Sir.'

I turned to look at Helmann.

Six foot three, shaven headed, with his Oberleutnant's cap, tailored in Berlin, pulled at a handsome angle over one eye. The Iron Cross on his neck, the breadth of his chest under his field-black panzer uniform, the MP 40 held over one shoulder. Also the faint tang of cognac, and the shadows under his grey, feline eyes.

'Our unit has fought superbly so far today, Faust,' he said. 'You yourself set an excellent example of determination.'

'Sir.'

I never heard him say such things before. Maybe it was his temporary promotion that made him so talkative, the Boss of our brigade being still stranded somewhere back on the steppe.

As if he read my thoughts, Helmann added,

'The Boss will hear about this. He'll be with us very soon.'

'Sir. I expect one of the Hanomags will bring up him and his crew.'

'Yes, yes.'

Helmann's grey eyes studied the plain behind our panzer, where the T34 defenders were still burning or lying in the mud, and our knocked-out Tigers were already being worked on by recovery teams, desperate to get the beasts hauled away for transport back to the salvage depots in the west.

'Here is the last Hanomag now,' Helmann said. 'I'm sure this is the Boss now.'

'Sir.'

We watched the final Hanomag approach slowly, picking its way through the craters and past the Russian fox holes. Our gunner and loader climbed down from the panzer, where they had been dumping out the spent shell cases and loading fresh stocks of 88mm and MG from a munitions tractor that accompanied the Hanomags.

Wilf, our gunner, was a wry, taciturn marksman who liked to live in the panzer. His mop of fair hair was shaved at the top to prevent it getting into his eyes. He spoke some of the Russian language, and he privately assured us that Russian women were possessed of wondrous appetites.

Stang, our 88mm gun loader and the fifth man of our crew, had suffered a head injury at Kharkov the year before; he rarely spoke except to acknowledge orders, but he was still the fastest 88mm breech man in the unit.

Up in our Tiger, my big, ugly comrade Kurt stood halfway out of his hatch, his radio headset still on – also watching the Hanomag approach.

The half-track came over the girder span, and clattered onto the mud of the ridge, steering around the debris and concrete that lay everywhere. It creaked to a halt beside us, and its commander, a young Captain, jumped down from the open hull, saluting Helmann.

'We have brought the Boss, Herr Ober,' the man said, in a cold voice.

'Yes, where is he? In the back? Is he ok?'

The Captain went around to the Hanomag's rear double doors, and hauled them open. We looked inside.

The Boss's Tiger crew were there – all of them – lying on the steel floor on the mud and ice. The Boss was among them. Like each of the others, he had a bullet wound in the forehead. It had blown the back of his skull away, and soaked his silver-grey hair with blood and brain matter. I noticed that his Iron Cross was missing.

'The Ivans must have caught them, Herr Ober,' the Captain said. 'Maybe the Reds were in a concealed slit trench. You see? They were executed, one after the other.'

Yes, it was obviously an execution. The men had been lined up and shot, one by one – that was evident. The Iron Cross had been taken as a souvenir. What other explanation was there?

I turned away from the sight, but I saw Helmann still examining the bodies, nodding to himself. Then he slammed the vehicle doors shut with a crash, and walked away, to where the gang of Russian radio team prisoners were huddled against the wall of the ruined bunker. Helmann took his MP40 quite casually off his shoulder, primed it, and shot five of the Russian prisoners, in the chest, one after the other.

The five survivors began to yell and plead for mercy in garbled voices. Only the coppery-haired woman soldier, whom Helmann had spared, remained silent, staring at the slumped corpses.

Helmann shouldered his weapon again, and lit a cigarette, studying the dead Russians in the way he had just studied the bodies of his dead comrades. Then he turned away and said to Wilf,

'Tell them to clean the tracks of my Panzer. I want all the *scheisse* off, and all the track links to be polished. Tell them in Russian to do that now.'

'Jawohl, Herr Ober.'

—

We knew something was wrong when we drove the Tiger up to the top of the ridge and looked down into the plain to the south. I had a pair of civilian binoculars that I always kept handy, and I used them to scan the low-lying land, feeling like a proper panzer chief.

'Well?' Kurt asked, both of us with our heads up out of our hatches, and the thick barrel of the 88mm over our heads against the freezing Russian sky. It was after midday, but the red sun still gave no heat. 'Where's the *Kampfgruppe?*'

I gave him the binoculars.

'There's nothing there,' he muttered. 'There's not a *scheisse* thing down there.'

'Maybe they're late?' I offered.

'Late?' he said. 'Well, some things *can* be late. Trams can be late, Faust – you know that. Easter is late some years. I had a pretty girlfriend once, who said she was two months late, when she wanted a ring on her finger. But a whole *Kamfgruppe?* Late?'

'Then why did we do all this?' I said. 'Why did we fight our way up here, and lose those men, and shoot all those *scheisse* Russians to bits?'

All along the ridge, on this piece of prime Soviet real estate bought so dearly, the other fifteen surviving Tiger crews, plus ten Hanomags full of Panzergrenadiers, were no doubt asking each other the same question – maybe not with my fine turn of phrase, though.

I could hear Helmann, still acting commander of the unit, having staccato discussions over the inefficient radio link with the Divisional commanders.

'*Wass?*' he was saying. 'When? How soon? How far? How many?'
Kurt and I exchanged a look.

Three minutes later, our newly-cleaned track links were thick
with Soviet mud, as we began to move, taking our prisoners with
us in the Hanomags. This time, though, we weren't advancing – we
were retreating, going back the way we came.

—

When I was a kid, in the 1930's, I used to listen to my dad, when he
came back from driving the tram, at the kitchen table in the little
apartment on Hofsee Strasse, by the railway line. He would tell me
stories about armies in victory and retreat – especially retreat.

Napoleon in Russia, the damned British in South Africa and
Ireland, and his own Kaiser Wilhelm army marching out of France
in 1919 with its rifles and artillery intact. I had the impression back
then, in our kitchen, that a retreat was a slow, orderly kind of affair –
with lots of lining up and queuing, and '*After you, Mein Herr!*' '*No,
after you, sir, I insist!*' along the way.

In the Wehrmacht, aged twenty, I learned that retreating in
Russia in 1943 was not like that. Retreating in Russia was pretty
much the same as advancing in Russia. It was at the same speed,
it was just as messy, and there were the same number of Reds after
your neck and your arse in its black Panzer trousers. The main dif-
ference was that the Reds were firing from behind you, not in front
of you; and therefore you couldn't look at them and drive at the
same time.

I couldn't tell my dad about this, of course, because the Allied
bombers flattened our apartment in Hofsee Strasse in 1942, and
killed my parents and my sister.

'Faust, what is wrong with you?'

I had just made the basic mistake of driving too close to a bomb
crater, and the earth had begun to give way under the right hand
tracks, forcing me to swerve left into a pile of debris from some
old Red tank. The bits of Russian steel clattered around in our

24

tracks, each one, I knew, a potential link-breaker that could leave us stranded until nightfall.

I felt Helmann's boot in my back, which I deserved.

'Keep it straight, man. Don't let me down.'

'Sir.'

'Keep it good and straight,' Kurt yelled over the bulkhead. 'Like a Munich tram.'

'Damn you, Kurt,' I muttered.

I kept it straight, though, at our column's steady 20kph, the same speed as the attack, each minute putting more ground between us and the counter-attacking Reds who were behind us. We were driving back across the steppe the way we had come, with the Russian winter sun declining in the west in front of us.

The fact was that we had to get back a long, long way beyond our initial assembly areas by the time that Soviet sun went down, or we were in all kinds of *scheisse*.

The fact was that the *Kampfgruppe* had failed in its mission to the south. Instead of us flanking and standing guard over their central assault, we were now isolated out on the steppe, alone in Ivan's own backyard, with, according to Helmann's briefing earlier...

'A regiment of Soviet armour, the new type, the JS tank. They're advancing on us from the north-west, and there's another pincer to the south east. Our *Kampfgruppe* are completely bogged down by PAK and minefields – our intelligence was wrong. Our objective now is to get back to the western river, to join up with the *Kampfgruppe* there, and hold the river bank on the eastern side against these Reds. If they get across the river, they'll swarm into the western plain. You know what that means.'

We knew.

The western plain had everything our army relied on: our salvage and repair depots, our hospitals, our logistics stations, our refitting points, our ammunition stocks, the railheads from the west, the airfields we needed. Above all, our precious, life-giving gasoline, in its underground, steel-lined chambers. If the Reds overran us on that western plateau...no gas, no ammunition, no supplies. The very borders of the Reich itself would be exposed to the Russian attack – an unimaginable concept. And our little column would turn into fifteen Tiger-shaped coffins, plus ten Hanomag-shaped hearses, deep inside a Soviet graveyard.

'It goes wrong sometimes,' Kurt yelled. 'Like love.'

'What do you know about love?'

'Plenty, my friend, plenty. Every time I get my pay.'

We were both head-up out of the hull hatches, sitting on our seat risers, our vehicle being in the centre of our column of armour. There were five Tigers at the front, then the ten Hanomags and their Panzergrenadiers, including the Soviet prisoners that we wanted to take back. Bringing up the rear were the final ten Tigers. We were the first of these, with the Hanomags in front of us. We were no longer in an arrowhead – but in a long, straight line of overheating machines, all running low on fuel.

Overhead, in the afternoon sky, I saw a pair of our beautiful Focke–Wulf fighters streak over us at about 500 metres altitude, also heading west, the black and white Reich crosses under their wings very clear in the light. One of them was trailing white smoke. Just as they passed over, another two aircraft swooped over us, with blue undersides – and the red star of Bolshevism clear on their wings. From my vision block, I saw them chase our FWs across the plain, and then, after barely half a minute, I saw a bright orange fire in the sky, and many puffs of white as explosions took place.

In a few seconds, the aerial combat above us became even clearer.

Our column left the open grasslands and regained the road leading out of the steppe – not a road in our proper German sense, but a flattened track with the luxury of stone chippings and occasional drainage ditches. As we mounted this roadway, I saw a shadow passing over our Tiger, a cross-shaped dark form. I glanced up, and saw a Stuka dive bomber flying very low, weaving from side to side and spitting out clouds of black fumes from its cowling. I saw that it was one of the new version Stukas – not a dive-bomber, but a tank-killer, with long cannon under its wings that could wreak havoc, so it was said, with the engine decks of any Russian armour.

This crooked-winged plane, with its wheel spats sticking down like claws, swooped across our column, lifted up, floated in the air a moment, with its engine pouring smoke – and then stalled and went down in a long belly-dive into the steppe. I saw it land away from the road, on our left, and I watched as broken bits of the tail-plane and wings flew out behind it. The entire propeller came spinning into our roadway, passing right in front of me, and crashed off to the other side.

I didn't stop, but the Hanomag in front of us did, and I had to swerve to avoid the *verdamm* thing. I could see down into its open interior, and I glimpsed the Russian prisoners huddled at the rear, faced by scowling Panzergrenadiers training guns on them. As the Hanomag slowed sharply, a gun went off – and one of the prisoners bucked and sprawled. I saw the Hanomag's rear doors open briefly – and the dead prisoner was thrown out onto the road. I guess the Tiger behind me ran him over – but by that point I was steering past the Hanomag off the road, and ploughing along the frozen Russian soil, while on my left the Stuka came to a rest and started to burn.

'We are not a transport for the Luftwaffe,' I heard Helmann say. 'But these pilots may have useful information. Faust, halt a moment.'

'Sir.'

I halted the Tiger.

To our left, out of the Stuka's smoke, I saw a man staggering towards us: an airman still in his flying helmet and blue overalls, with his arm around a wounded comrade who was stumbling and dragging his feet, evidently in the last stages of consciousness. Behind them, the Stuka's cannon rounds exploded in spirals of white sparks, and the glass canopy blew open in the gasoline fire.

The Stuka airman saw our vehicle waiting for him, and a Tiger must have looked like a vision of rescue, because he dropped his unconscious comrade and ran to us. Standing at the roadside, he saluted and shouted up at Helmann in the cupola,

'Take me on board, comrades. The Reds are ten kilometres behind you here.'

'Come up here and brief me on the situation,' Helmann shouted. 'What about your friend there?'

'He is dead, Herr Ober.'

Ten seconds after that, we were rolling again, and the pilot was crammed into the turret cage with Helmann, Wilf the gunner, and Stang the breech-man, telling our commander what he knew of the Red advance. I went down into the hull compartment and closed the hatch, so that I could listen in while driving.

'There are fifty of those new Josef Stalin tanks behind us,' the Luftwaffe man was saying with excitement. 'Those big monsters are like solid iron. Our Stuka cannons can damage them in the engine grilles, but on the turrets we hardly make a dent on them. I can tell you, I shot them up until I had no cannon shells left.'

'You had cannon shells left when you crashed just now,' Helmann said. 'I saw them exploding. But what direction are the Reds going, and what forces do they have with them?'

'They are heading for the western river, Herr Oberleutnant. Straight for the river. They're going at speed, too. They'll cross this road in half an hour, I'd say. They have mobile artillery, and infantry in trucks, about fifty trucks of them. I *may* have had some ammunition left,' he added. 'But you see, it does so little against those Stalins.'

'Which is your airbase?'

'Plovenka, to the west of the river. If that is overrun by these Ivan tanks, there'll be no air cover for a hundred kilometre radius.'

Kurt and I grinned at each other over the bulkhead; the unreliability of the Luftwaffe in providing air protection was already a grim joke among panzer boys throughout the East.

Helmann questioned the airman further, but he seemed to know little else of use to us. We rejoined our armoured column at the rear, tucking in behind the Hanomag holding the prisoners, and we transferred the pilot across to that same vehicle. The pilot seemed to think this was below his dignity, but he had no choice in the matter.

We rolled on towards the river on the western horizon. We were fifteen Tigers and ten Hanomag half-tracks, the best machines in the world for their purpose, but we were outnumbered.

—

Just as the sun touched the western land, I saw Russians south of us. They were a row of dark shapes in the distant steppe, trailing exhaust fumes, surrounded by showers of mud spray. Helmann had already seen them, because he was on the radio link to the other Tigers, ordering them to turn and fight.

'They shouldn't be there this soon,' Kurt said, as I turned the Tiger to face the oncoming Ivans.

'This is an advance group, I'm sure of that,' Helmann said in our headphones, as I brought the panzer to a halt in an area of low, grassy dunes off the road. 'This is just a sample of what's on offer. We must fight them off, and then we will resume our march.'

On our right, the other Tigers were taking up position also, in groups of two or three over a perimeter of several kilometres. The Hanomags grouped up on the ground behind them, seeking what cover they could among the low mounds of frozen grass. It was better for them to stay with us than strike out on their own and encounter more Red armour on the way.

I saw the Russian vehicles more clearly: a line of a maybe dozen abreast, low and squat in appearance, much wider than a T34. These were the new Stalin tanks, for sure, and in the sky above them, over their fumes…

'Aircraft,' Helmann cursed. 'Red planes. Sturmoviks.'

I felt my throat tighten in fear. Sturmoviks were Russian fighter-bombers, slow but protected with armour plate on their bellies, and they loved nothing more than strafing German boys with their cannons and bomb-loads. I could see them up in the corner of my cracked vision block, three little dots against the reddening sky, issuing vapour as they descended on us.

'They'll make an attack, and then the Stalins will come in,' Helmann said on the radio to the other Tiger commanders. 'Be ready for this.'

I could see the prisoners' Hanomag near us, concealed behind a dune, with a soldier in the cab lining up an MG 42 into the air. A fine gun, the '42, putting out a thousand rounds per minute – but what use was it against Sturmoviks and Stalins? If the soldier also had such doubt, he didn't show them – he fired off a burst of tracer to assess the distance, and then, like everyone else, he waited while the Sturmoviks descended and the Stalins advanced.

The seconds were long and painful. My mouth was dry and my heart was thumping in rhythm with the Maybach transmission, seeing the planes come lower, closer now than the Stalin tanks below them. Then the aircraft were on us, and the Hanomag soldier opened up with his MG as they swooped in.

The Sturmoviks' wings flickered with cannon, and I saw the front of the Hanomag blow apart as the shells went through its thin armour. The visored windows split open, and the soldier on the MG42 was ripped to pieces, thrown out of the vehicle bodily as the cannon shells tore in. The Hanomag's rear doors flew open, and that copper-haired Ivan girl threw herself out onto the ground, her hands over her head. Our Luftwaffe pilot friend emerged, and threw himself down beside her.

The cannons hit our Tiger as well, each impact like a hammer on our steel body, and immediately they dropped their bombs. I saw two small, tear-shaped bombs shoot down almost horizontally in their trajectory, one landing near a Tiger and showering it with earth and mud. The other fell behind a dune – and as it exploded, I saw pieces of another Hanomag and its troops whirling through the air – wheels, bits of track, men's bodies and sheets of metal plate, all trailing smoke and flames.

The planes were gone as quickly as they appeared, and while debris was still falling to the ground, our Tigers opened fire on the Stalins.

The range was some two kilometres, but it was better to keep these beasts at a distance, not let them get close. Our 88mm gun boomed, and the familiar reek of propellant charge filled the hull. I saw our tracer rounds shooting out all along our line, the high velocity taking just a fraction of a second to reach the Russians.

We hit two of the Stalins straight away, one of them immediately trailing a plume of fire as it slowed to a halt, and the other slewing around as its track was shed, presenting its side armour inadvertently. One of our gunners took the invitation, and put a round clean into the hull above the wheels. The Red tank crawled slowly, smouldering, and then began to burn from the rear deck.

These tanks were massive, though – wider even than our Tigers, equipped with a huge, oblong turret – and while we knocked down those two, I also saw our rounds hit their Red comrades and ricochet off completely, spinning off across the steppe into the distance. One of the Stalins was hit twice, then three times, and each shell was deflected in this way, bouncing right off the turret or glacis plate.

'*Scheisse*,' Kurt observed – and he was right. We really were deep in it.

When the Stalins returned fire, their muzzles spat out orange flames straight at us. There was a colossal impact on our front plate, and our sixty-tonne panzer shuddered under the blow. Up in the turret, Wilf kept firing, the shell cases raining down out of the breech onto the hull floor. The Tiger nearest us was hit in the turret, and I saw the great, steel structure lift out of its bearings for a second, and then judder as the gunner's hatch flew open and sheets of sparks and smoke came out.

The commander's cupola hatch slid open over the side of the turret, and the commander appeared, struggling to escape the inferno that must be erupting inside. He was trapped, though, and he writhed as the flames below grew so fierce that they rose three metres out of the gunner's hatch beside him. Down on the hull, the driver's hatch opened – the man in there sitting exactly where I was in my own panzer – and two arms appeared, as the driver sought to haul himself out. His arms remained there, lifeless, as smoke and flames poured from his hatch also.

On the ground by the wrecked Hanomag, I saw the red-haired Russian woman looking around desperately as the panzer battle erupted over her, surrounded as she was by the smouldering bodies of her captors and her fellow prisoners. I saw Kurt hunch over his machine gun and take aim at her.

'No,' I said. 'Leave her.'

He looked at me and shrugged.

'Get us behind one of those dunes, Faust,' Helmann shouted. 'We can shoot over the top.'

I drove the Tiger over to the nearest dune, a low mound of frozen tundra, and brought it to a halt on top of the mechanical and human wreckage of a bombed-out Hanomag. Its crew were beyond help now, and we needed the added shelter of the mound which marked their final stopping point.

Our turret traversed left, and continued firing, with the dune guarding our hull side. In this new location, I could see right along our line of panzers, our Tigers stretching into the distance, pouring out their fire on the attackers. I saw the nearest Tiger take a hit in the front track, sending shattered links soaring into the smoky air, their steel reflecting the setting sun. He was hit again in the flank; the round penetrated and then came shooting out of the engine grilles, having evidently rebounded inside the crew compartment. Bits of the engine flew out in sparks, and burning gasoline began to erupt from the tanks, flooding the whole panzer in orange flames. I hoped the crew were dead before the fuel poured down into the hull.

On my left, two of the Stalins were manoeuvring at high speed to outflank us and fire along our line from that angle. Several of our Tigers traversed their turrets to aim at this threat, and they shot up the leading Stalin by blowing off his tracks on both sides. I saw the huge Russian vehicle flop down in the mud, and continue sliding on its belly, carried by its momentum towards the Tigers, still firing, even though tracks and wheels were flying out behind it.

It came to rest at point-blank range in front of a Tiger, which lowered its barrel and finished the crippled JS with two rounds through the upper hull. The Russian's hatches were blown off, and the turret began to spin around, issuing sparks from the gun muzzle. The crewmen who scrambled out were blown apart by a high explosive shell from the Tiger, their limbs scattering across their steppe.

That second Stalin of the pair, though, had broken through, and he came crashing over the hillocks between our panzers, firing at a rapid rate against anything with a German cross on its side. A Hanomag was hit as it tried to reverse away, and the whole half-track stood up on its armoured nose, its tracks racing around in the air and the Panzergrenadiers inside falling out, until their vehicle thumped down on top of them, and exploded in a wave of burning fuel.

Two Tigers engaged that one JS, and even at close range I saw their shells deflect repeatedly from that massive turret, while the Russian hit one Tiger in the gun mantle, causing the 88mm gun to slump onto the front deck, with smoke coming from the turret ring. The disarmed panzer sought to retreat by retreating, but reversed clumsily into a crater, allowing its underside to ride up in full view of the Stalin. The Red gunner sent his shell cleanly through the belly plate, and the Tiger convulsed as its stored ammunition evidently exploded, making the whole turret spin off, dragging the turret crew with it in their burning cage.

The second Tiger stood its ground, and with great coolness shot away the Stalin's left track at a range of 100 metres. Before the Stalin could traverse its gun, the Tiger rolled around to stand at the Stalin's rear, where the back plate of any armoured vehicle is thinner and lighter over the engine. The Stalin tried to crawl away, but its broken track bunched up and hobbled it, so that it could only move a few metres in the mud. The Tiger put a single round through the Stalin's back plate, splitting it open in a shower of rivets. The Stalin's crew continued to traverse the turret, until the whole vehicle was on fire from spilled fuel, and the Tiger reversed to find another opponent in the melee.

Up in our turret, Helmann was barking orders to the other commanders, as the tank battle became a close-quarters and mobile scrap, like a street fight - but a fight between men armed with steel carapaces and the most powerful guns their nations could supply.

'Outflank them to the left, driver,' he yelled at me. 'Left and to their side, let them come through us,' he shouted, as I threw the Maybach into gear and the transmission spat its burning lubricant into my face. 'That's the way!'

All along our line, the Tigers were breaking position, swerving left and right to present highly mobile targets to the onrushing six or seven Stalins that still faced us. The little Hanomags tried to escape in some cases – but the Stalins saw them as soon as they broke their cover among the tundra dunes, and shot them with high-explosive that ripped their angled sides open. In other cases, the Panzergrenadiers leapt from their transports and found cover among the dunes, waiting for the tank battle to somehow burn out.

I lost sight of the Russian woman prisoner and the Luftwaffe pilot, who I last saw still flattening their faces into the mud and ice, with their hands over their heads.

I drove the Tiger, sliding on the ice, out of the protection of the hillocks, and slewed it around so that we faced the Stalins from the side. One of the Red machines, barely a hundred metres distant, surely noticed our movement – because it rotated its hull until its front plate, a colossal wall of steel, was facing directly onto us. Wilf, up in our turret, fired three times in ten seconds, with Stang our breech-man grunting as he reloaded with amazing speed each time. Our rounds deflected off the Stalin's huge turret twice – and the third actually stuck in the armour plate, a slug of German steel jammed into a slab of Russian steel, its tracer still glowing red.

Beyond the Stalin, I saw a Tiger roll into a depression in the ground, burning from the engine deck; and then another of our panzers standing still, with its hatches open and the crew climbing out with their uniforms on fire.

Suddenly, my glass vision block shattered as we were hit on our front plate by the Stalin facing us. I heard another impact striking our turret, and a long groan from somebody up there, followed by a series of shouted commands from Helmann. Yet another impact came, low on our front hull, and the blow threw me back in my seat. My ears were ringing, and I could see nothing through the wrecked glass except the red sunset sky, in broken fragments.

I felt Helmann kick me in the back, and the tip of his polished boot brought me to my senses.

In the seat alongside me, Kurt was yelling,

'Push out the glass, Faust, for the sake of *scheisse*. Helmann's telling you to ram that Stalin. Ram it!'

In a daze, I unclamped the vision block from inside, raised the armoured bracket and pushed the broken glass out onto the hull front. A blast of freezing air came in, bringing smoke and sprays of ice - and then a blast of metal fragments as another shell hit us, blowing scabs of armour plate off our front.

With bits of metal in my face, I drove the Tiger straight at the Stalin, aiming hull-to-hull across the rolling ground. I could not understand why our gun was not firing – but that terrible groan which erupted when the Stalin's shell hit us told me someone in the turret was badly wounded. With no gun, we could only use our sixty tonnes and our Maybach as a battering ram – it was either that, or sit obediently and be shot to pieces.

We covered the hundred metres between us and the Russian in seconds, moving so fast that the Stalin gunner could not calibrate on us and shot right past us twice, his orange tracer lighting up the dark, frozen earth. I eased off the throttle as we approached the prow of the Stalin, and our Tiger tracks bit into the tundra; the running gear began howling and the belly of the panzer started slamming up and down as we slid – effectively out of control now – directly into the Ivan machine.

I heard Kurt curse, and I saw him brace with his hands over his skull – and at the last moment I did the same, with the steel glacis of the JS filling my entire vision. The impact was like a kick in the belly, and after that, it took me a few seconds to realise what was happening.

We were stationary, wedged up against the Stalin; the Russian panzer seemed to have stalled in the concussion too, because there was no engine noise from outside at all. Then I realised that our Tiger too had cut out, and I tried to restart our motor frantically with the hand switch. I could still hear that groaning voice from our turret, and a muttered dialogue between Wilf and Helmann, who were trying to use the hand crank to operate the turret.

I saw our 88mm barrel swing slowly around and depress in elevation, coming down over my head and pointing straight into the Stalin's upper deck. I could actually see into the JS driver's position through his vision slit – his lights were still on inside, and men were moving around in there, maybe struggling to restart their engine.

In the next moment, we fired.

I clearly saw our armour-piercing round burst through their upper armour, and enter inside the compartment. Through the Russian's vision slit, I saw our warhead ricochet again and again inside there, flying chaotically around the confined space and bouncing off the steel walls, glowing bright red. Finally, the explosive charge in the projectile detonated, in a plume of sparks. I saw nothing more inside there, as smoke filled the interior.

We were so close that the recoil of our gun had pushed us back a metre from the other tank, but still our engine would not catch. Up on top of the Stalin's turret, two men climbed out of their hatches, their backs and sleeves smouldering with flames. Both had machine pistols with a cylinder magazine – and without even hesitating, these two Ivans jumped straight from their wrecked vehicle onto our battered but still functioning Tiger.

Kurt fired on them with his gimbal MG, but the smouldering Russians were already on our roof and impossible to hit. I heard them moving above me, their boots clunking on the armour plate as they clambered up onto our turret. In the turret, Wilf fired his co-axial MG, and I saw the body of one Russian crash down onto the front hull in front of my vision port. There was shooting from outside the turret, and I heard Helmann yelling, 'He's shooting into the engine!'

Was that to be our destiny? To have our Tiger set ablaze by a Russian emptying his machine gun through our engine grilles, incinerating himself as he set us on fire too? No!

Our engine finally caught life and started, and I reversed the panzer with a great jolt, to dislodge whoever was up there. I saw that second tank man thrown forwards off the turret by the movement; he fell onto the ground in front of us, still clutching his gun and with his uniform still on fire. I drove forwards over him, traversing the tank across him to make sure he was finished, and then I advanced back into the scrum of fighting vehicles.

I saw that the engagement was in its final stages.

Of our fifteen Tigers, I could see several burning, and of our ten Hanomags, I saw at least five lying destroyed among the undulating ground. The Stalins were reduced to a handful, who were now seeking to retreat, leaving the rest of their dozen on fire, or wrecked and static. The setting sun was touching the western horizon now, exactly where we wanted to be heading: a molten red disc surrounded by streaks of gold and purple cloud. Its light slanted across the battlefield, showing its mayhem in stark detail.

I saw the crew of a Tiger burning up with their vehicle – each man slumped in his hatch, presumably killed by a high-explosive burst as they tried to escape. The flames rose around them, fed by their gasoline reserves, a column of orange as high as an oak tree against the sunset. I saw the crew of a Stalin, disembarked from their bogged-down vehicle in a crater, being set upon by Panzergrenadiers from a Hanomag. Our troops were venting their anger and frustration, and yet conserving their precious ammunition, by bayoneting the Russian crews and clubbing them down with entrenching spades.

I drove our Tiger back between the low hills, with Wilf in the turret firing occasional shots at the retreating Stalins – firing so slowly that I knew that something was wrong with our gun or with our turret crew.

All along our remaining line of Tigers, the firing was coming to a stop, as crews guarded their ammunition, not expending it on a withdrawing enemy. I drove us back to where we had begun the battle, where the prisoner Hanomag had been hit. Rounding one of the low hills, I saw a sight that made no sense at all.

There were Russian infantry here.

Where the *scheisse* had they come from?

There were three tall, tough-looking Russian soldiers – not tank crew, but heavily-armed ground troops, picking their way across the ice and mud, holding heavy-calibre automatic weapons, and looking as if they were searching for something, as if they were looking for something among all the debris and wreckage of the Hanomags.

Beside me, Kurt opened fire on them immediately, knocking down two of them, leaving their bodies wreathed in smoke. Kurt's MG34 clicked empty, though – and he scrabbled around for a fresh magazine, cursing eloquently.

The remaining Ivan soldier took a look at us, seemed to judge the situation, and ducked in between two of the dunes to escape. I drove the Tiger fast around the low rises of earth, and turning the corner after that, I came face to face with another Stalin tank.

The soldier we had shot at was vaulting into it, disappearing into the hull hatch, and the vehicle was vibrating as the engine revved up. Its huge gun barrel traversed a fraction, to face directly into our turret. Why did we not fire? I glanced around to look at the turret cage – and saw from its position that it was traversed way over to the other side, our gun pointing in completely the wrong direction to fire at this vehicle. Reversing would do no good either; the Russian gun was already directly on us.

I rested my head on the control wheel, and waited for the impact of the Russian shell. I had just seen in that other Stalin the way a projectile flew around inside a crew compartment, slashing and ripping whatever it hit.

A second passed, and I heard the JS engine crash into gear, and then rattle away from us. I looked up, and the tank still had its gun pointing at us, like a bank robber who coolly retreats down the street while pointing his revolver at the guards. In this way, he was saving himself from being set upon by all our furious Tigers at once, and so ensuring that he lived to tell the story.

I watched him go – the last one of the great Stalins, getting smaller as he finally span around and roared away in forward gear, disappearing into the dusk of the steppe.

What the *scheisse* was that about?

I clambered around, wriggled through the bulkhead behind my seat and peered up into the turret. Wilf, our gunner, still had his face to the gun sight. Stang, our loader, however, was slumped against the turret bars, with blood pouring from his neck. Helmann was taking a long drink from a hip flask. He threw it down to me, and Kurt and I shared a swig.

'What's happened to Stang?' I said.

'We need a new loader,' Helmann muttered. 'And we need to get moving.'

———

Stang had been killed when a Stalin shell struck the side of the turret. Although the shell didn't penetrate, the shock wave blasted a scab of metal off the inside of the turret wall, which severed the back of Stang's spinal cord at the base of the skull. We placed him on the frozen ground, together with our dead Panzergrenadiers.

Living men driven by foreboding of death, we hurried to regroup from our losses, reorganising our destroyed panzers, our half-tracks and men. We had lost seven Tigers in all, leaving only eight Tigers remaining now, plus four Hanomags and their crews of

Panzergrenadiers, plus the Russian prisoner woman. All her companions had been killed by the Sturmovik assault on their transport. She remained alone, her red hair streaked with ice, rocking herself back and forth as she stood in the tundra. We put her in a working Hanomag with our wounded, the poor souls who lacked medical care or even basic pain relief. In with them went our Luftwaffe friend; his elegant one-piece flying suit now drenched in mud.

This was a time of frantic activity, with no chance to reflect or discuss the battle in depth. We checked the panzers' running gear, and decided we could press on for twenty or thirty kilometres, in order to put space and darkness between us and the main body of Ivans advancing on us from the north. We left our panzer dead in their vehicles, burning like Vikings, and we withdrew from that evil place with its dunes and smashed bodies.

Back on the road of crushed stones, in the ice and mud, we formed a slow column of four Tigers in the lead, then the four Hanomags, and the last four remaining panzers bringing up the rear, with their turrets traversed to face backwards in case the enemy caught up as we retreated. Several times, we heard aircraft overhead, swooping low, but by then we were swallowed up in the night of the endless plain, shielded by darkness.

It was hopeless to try to continue the journey in the dark. Driving a panzer at night, with no lights, is almost impossible, and an invitation to wreck the vehicle. Each driver followed the exhaust glow of the panzer in front, keeping fifty metres of space to avoid collisions, progressing at only ten kph because of the danger of hitting obstacles or ditches that could finish us.

Helmann said that he had found us a place on the map, where we might wait for a few hours and make repairs to our vehicles. At first light, we would then need a sustained drive, using all our remaining fuel, to reach the western river and help in its defence against the onslaught.

In this way, bunching and halting, cursing ourselves and each other, with our minds still buzzing from the intense combat, we entered a shallow valley away from the road. A moon was rising, the colour of gunmetal, but it seemed to give almost no light at all. In the darkness, we steered to a halt on Helmann's command: four Tigers in front, then four Hanomags, and then the final four Tigers.

We cut our engines, while a team of Panzergrenadiers went ahead on foot to investigate the valley. As the clump of their boots on the frozen ground faded, I listened to the engine bulkhead clicking as it cooled, and the impatient tap of Helmann's boot against the turret. Fog grew around us, sparkling with ice crystals. When the Panzergrenadiers returned, Helmann climbed down to consult with them, standing in front of the panzer. I opened my hatch slightly to hear their voices.

'Well? Is the zone safe?'

'It seems to be safe, Herr Ober. The valley goes on for two hundred metres, and the road is passable. It is rough, but frozen hard. We saw no sign of the enemy.'

'Then we will stop here.'

'And also, sir, we have found, as you see…'

The soldier stood to one side. Behind him, emerging from the fog, wearing greatcoats, faces not quite obscured in scarves were…

Kurt whistled in appreciation.

'German nurses,' he said. 'What are two fine young German nurses doing here, eh?'

Helmann introduced himself – then asked the women the same question.

'We are with the German Red Cross, Herr Oberleutnant,' one of them said, in a Berlin accent. The red symbol on her white dress was very prominent under her oversized greatcoat. 'Our hospital was evacuated in the retreat, but we were left behind. We are very eager to accompany you. We must not be left to the Reds. Please.'

'Well, our wounded men need attention. Have you ever been in a Hanomag?' Helmann asked.

'Never, Herr Oberleutnant.'

'Then this shall be your first time, ladies.'

'First time for everything,' Kurt said, winking at me.

—

As the nurses boarded the Hanomag which contained the wounded and the surviving Russian prisoner, we panzer crews climbed down from our machines and looked around.

We were in a valley with broad slopes, well-hidden from the steppe above. There were a few indistinct shapes of trees, some large boulders, but nothing else visible. The time was precious, and, using torches with black shields to minimise the light, each crew set to work to maintain their vehicle before the renewed march.

Our Tigers were never designed to drive sustained journeys, not even on smooth city roads. The stress and wear to the running gear was too great, and the entire engine and transmission itself only lasted for 1,000 kilometres before being completely replaced. Several of our panzers were at that point now, and their crews muttered gloomily about the prospects of them finishing the journey at all without burning out or seizing up. Even the track links – those great chunks of steel weighing ten kilos each – wear quickly under the duress, and the tracks must be tightened and adjusted if the track is not to snap or become tangled on the drive wheels. The pins that hold these links together are thick steel rods, as heavy as the poker from your grandfather's fireplace – but they eventually bend under the massive strain, and if just one pin breaks apart, the whole sixty tonne panzer can be stranded and helpless.

Together with Wilf and Kurt, I checked along our track length, seeing beyond the mud and debris of human flesh that the treads had collected again, to assess its integrity. Our link pins were looking distorted and loose.

'Well?' Helmann asked, appearing behind me. He was like a cat, moving silently on his clean heels, with his grey eyes always watching us.

'We might make another fifty kilometres on these tracks, Herr Ober,' I said. 'Then we'll have to strip off the treads and replace the pins. See how they buckle? They're wearing badly. I think the metal is lower quality than usual.'

'The steel must last,' Helmann said. 'It's a hundred kilometres to the river, Faust. We have fuel for exactly one hundred kilometres. We must reach the river, we are needed there for its defence. And maybe we can pick up more fuel at some point on the way.'

'Sir.'

I switched off my torch, and we stood in the freezing dark, hunched over, hands in our pockets. To take a Tiger one hundred kilometres, with barely enough fuel, being chased by vengeful Russians equipped with a whole army of those damned Stalin monsters.

'We'll make it, though, won't we?' a voice said.

This was our muddy Luftwaffe pilot, standing near us in the dark.

'Ah, you are the pilot who shot off all his ammunition,' Helmann observed. 'I'm glad you are here with us.'

'Indeed, Herr Ober?'

'Indeed,' Helmann purred. 'You're a strong fellow, with a fine set of shoulders.'

'I am the *Geschwader* boxing champion.'

'Excellent, excellent. We need a man such as you, to be the loader for our 88mm.'

'Me? A panzer gun loader?' the pilot spluttered. 'But I am not trained on such a weapon.'

'Wilf shall train you,' Helmann said, slapping both men on the back. 'It will take an hour or so. Then you will get some rest, because we move again at first light. Continue, please.'

—

While Wilf and the pilot were up in the turret going through the breech loading procedure, Helmann held a short conference, further up the road, with his seven remaining Tiger commanders. Left alone with Kurt, I opened a tin of ration meat and ate half of it. The meat was weird-tasting – it was old army horse, some people said, or even donkey. Whatever its origin, I chewed the stuff down rapidly, leaning against the front plate of our Tiger. The panzer's steel was solid under my elbow, and I took comfort from its weight. Then I put the remaining ration away for later on, and Kurt lit a cigarette which we shared.

'Well, that was quite a little battle we had back there,' Kurt said.

I blew a plume of smoke from my nose, thinking back over the engagement among the dunes on the steppe. Throughout history, I believe, every man who has been in combat has felt the need to discuss it afterwards, to reflect and share its memories, to rejoice, to commiserate and perhaps to learn the lessons from it. It is a primitive male instinct, as strong as the sexual urge. To deny soldiers this shared memory would be like an imprisonment, like the amputation of his tongue.

We talked for some time – reliving the battle in this way, and for these reasons, in our minds.

'You know what was the strangest thing?' Kurt said.

'Was it when you whimpered like a Fraulein?'

His big, ugly face broke into a grin.

'No, my big hero. It was those three Ivan foot soldiers who came out of that Stalin tank at the end.'

'How do you know they came out of that Stalin?'

'One of them jumped back inside there, didn't he?' Kurt threw his cigarette away. 'So they must have come from in there. Where else did they appear from – was it the healthy Russian air?'

'But how could three big Red soldier boys be riding around in a panzer?'

'Well, they'd have to cut down on all the ammunition storage, just to fit them in there,' Wilf mused. 'Maybe that's one reason why he didn't fire on us at the end.'

'Maybe. But why take those three infantry guys along at all? And why were they prowling around in the dunes there? They weren't attacking us. It was almost as if they were *looking* for something.'

'Russia's a strange place,' Wilf said philosophically. 'Things happen, and nobody knows why.'

'I'll tell you one thing,' I said. 'Those JS tanks are superb machines. If they break through across the river and start driving to the west...'

'We shall stop them,' Helmann said behind us, evidently coming back from his conference. I wasn't sure how long he'd been standing in the shadows, listening to our conversation. 'With *our* superb machines,' he went on, 'we will hold the river crossing, I promise you. And now we have a new gun loader. A boxing champion, too!'

'Everything's fine, then, sir.' Kurt stood up straight. 'Your orders?'

'Send this to Divisional command in code,' Helmann said, giving him a slip of paper. 'Send it once only, we do not wish to have Ivans locating our radio position.'

As Kurt was manning his radio set in the hull, Helmann kept me standing outside.

'You drove the panzer well today, Faust.'

'Sir.'

'I heard you just now, speculating about those three Ivan ground troops that we saw.'

'It seemed very unusual, sir.'

'I agree that it was unusual. It was really quite *unheimlich*.' That was one of his favourite words, meaning it was suspicious, strange or threatening. 'And what do you think that they were doing there?'

'They were there with a purpose, sir, that was evident.'

'That was the impression I had also.' Helmann frowned, pursing his lips. 'And they were near the prisoner Hanomag, were they not?'

'I suppose they were, Herr Ober.'

'And our prisoners were a radio signals team, which is why we were holding onto them. They may have had important intelligence for our interrogators. Although there is only one of them left now... just that woman.'

Helmann took off his tailored officer's cap, and rubbed his cropped hair. In the faint moonlight, he looked pale and tense. He had over his shoulder the MP40 that he had used to kill the prisoners at the bunker, and his hand moved to it, perhaps unconsciously.

'We have a little time of darkness before we move,' he said. 'Let's use the time to interrogate the prisoner. Bring the woman into the Tiger where we can see her in the electric light. That will make an impression on her. Also, Wilf speaks some Russian. He can be my interpreter.'

—

I found the woman prisoner in one of the Hanomags, hunched up on one of the seats among the wounded, while the two German nurses did what they could to ease the injured men's suffering. I saw that they had a satchel of morphine capsules, and they were administering these readily, giving the soldiers much-needed sleep. The two girls were already discussing what they would do that night, once all the wounded were taken care of. They looked at me and winked.

I took the Russian woman to our panzer, and sent her down into the turret through the gunner's hatch. I climbed in through my driver's hatch, and crouched at the base of the turret cage, listening to the interrogation. The Luftwaffe man crouched opposite me on the hull floor, to make space for the Helmann, Wilf and the woman up there.

'What is your name?' Helmann asked, and Wilf translated the question in hesitant Russian.

In reply, she gave a name which had a long patronymic.

'What is your role in your army?'

Again Wilf made the translation, and then he translated her reply.

'Herr Ober, she says that she is a junior signals operator.'

'Why was she at the bunkers?'

The translation came again.

46

'She says that she was there with a team of operators, who are now dead, and they were there to send simple radio messages. She says she is not a combat soldier, and she asks for humane treatment. She says she has not eaten for twenty-four hours.'

Helmann's chuckle made the hairs on my neck stand up. It was *unheimlich.*

'What type of messages did her radio team know how to send?'

'She says their messages were basic field requests at a local company level.'

'Really?'

I saw Helmann look into her eyes for a long time. I couldn't see her face up there, but I could hear her breathing, which was much faster and lighter than our men's breathing.

'Now ask her which codes she has a knowledge of, whether encrypted by hand or by machine, and what encryptions she can formulate and decipher.'

Wilf struggled to ask the question in his basic Russian, and the woman sounded confused as she answered.

'I think she's saying that she has no knowledge of encryption. She has not used any encryption machines, she says.'

'Tell her to show me her hands. That's right. Now ask her why her hands are so very smooth and unmarked.'

'She says she only uses a pen and pencil, she does not do lifting and carrying.'

'So, we've found the one girl in Russia who does not do lifting and carrying. I've seen Russian girl troops lifting twenty-kilo sandbags all day. They're born to it.'

'Do you want me to translate that, Herr Ober?'

'No. Just ask her if she has friends in the Red Army.'

A complex translation followed.

'She says she does not understand the question, sir.'

I could see the woman's feet on the platform of the cage above me. One of her ankles was trembling. The Luftwaffe man opposite me noticed that too, and raised an eyebrow.

'Ask her,' Helmann instructed, 'if she knows important people, officers, who might want to protect her and her radio team, and why they might want to do this this.'

'She says she knows no important officers, and she is a basic radio clerk.'

Helmann slapped the woman in the face.

The sound echoed around inside the panzer's bare metal surfaces, and the woman's stifled cry echoed slightly too. The pilot looked at me with a grin, and I hated him from then on.

'Tell her,' Helmann said, 'that we are too busy to get the truth from her right now. But if she has any important knowledge, she is being very foolish. Our colleagues in the intelligence services will interrogate her when we hand her over to them, and they are not gentlemen like us. We are in a hurry, but they will take their time with her. Assure her of this.'

The hesitant translation took some time.

'She says she is a radio clerk, from a basic radio team, and she has not eaten.'

'Enough. Put her in the Hanomag, with a double guard. Two armed men, to watch her at all times. Then at first light – *Panzer Marsch.*'

I took the woman back to the Hanomag. She was breathing sharply, and there was blood on her chin from where Helmann hit her. She stopped in the darkness to wipe it, talking to herself in Russian, breathlessly. Her hair came loose, and I saw that even in the dim moonlight it was long and thick, in coils over her shoulders. I could smell the clean, female scent of her hair, a scent which I had long forgotten.

On an impulse, I gave her my remaining half tin of army meat and my fork. She took it and ate quickly, devouring it. I gave her a piece of sugar from my pocket, and a drink of water from my flask, and she gulped at that.

She said something to me in Russian, which I didn't understand.

I took her back to the Hanomags.

The wounded were sleeping through their morphine in their allotted vehicle, the open roof being covered over with a tarpaulin on which were laid branches and snow, so that the compartment was at least roughly sealed against the weather. Inside, a small kerosene stove was burning with a steady heat. The two nurses were nowhere to be seen there.

The adjacent Hanomag, however, looked very welcoming. The troops had spread a tarpaulin over this one too, and another small stove was burning inside. The nurses were holding court in there, entertaining various Panzergrenadiers and tank crew with a lot of friendly conversation.

I took two of these infantry men aside and relayed Helmann's orders about putting a double guard on the Russian woman. They took the Russian to another Hanomag, which was covered over in the same way but not heated, and they put her inside this vehicle. I got the men to light a stove for her, and she smiled in gratitude. She curled up on the bench and put her hands over her head. The two men stood guard over her, casting impatient glances over at the nurses' Hanomag.

Outside that one, a queue was forming.

—

Our Tiger was warm inside – being no more than one or two degrees below freezing. We had a ceramic cylinder heater which was warmed from the engine while it was running, and then radiated heat for an hour or so while the engine was still. We were lucky in this respect. We called the ground troops *the icicle soldiers*, because of the frozen snot and tears that we often saw projecting from their faces. On the other hand, when our ceramic cylinder eventually went cold, we were stuck and unable to move our limbs in the freezing panzer, while the infantry could at least light their kerosene stoves and move their feet.

I didn't sleep, but I imagined a few sweet things. I imagined being around the kitchen table at home, before the war started, with the oven glowing, and my mother at the radio, tuning the dial. Before the war, she loved to hear the different languages that the wireless picked up, the Italian and French and Danish.

'So many people in the world,' she would say in admiration. 'Can you hear them? So many people.'

I shook my head, coming back to reality. I wiped down my vision block and checked the tension in the transmission gear selector. It was running loose.

Kurt came back into the panzer some time later, through his hatch, and chuckled to himself as he closed it.

'Ah, but those nurses are experts at treating a male patient,' he said. 'The brunette one cured me in no time at all.'

'Cured you of what?'

'My needs,' he yawned in a cloud of vapour, and settled back in his seat. 'She gave me the old Berlin handshake. I paid with a piece of sugar, so we were both happy.'

'I'm surprised you didn't pay with a piece of sausage.'

He laughed, and in the dim light I saw him stroking the flank of his machine gun.

'The other lads paid with sausage, and with cigarettes, and dried apple, brandy, and everything a woman could wish for,' he said. 'My God, but those nurses ate and drank well tonight. They will sleep like true angels.'

It was quiet in the hull, with just the sound of our breathing.

'By the way – about those two nurses,' Kurt said in a sleepy way. 'They have a Walther pistol with them. They say it's in case the Red soldiers capture them. They'd rather kill themselves with a bullet in the head than be violated by the Reds. They showed me the gun – they know how to use it, and they mean it, too.' He yawned. 'They really will shoot themselves, in preference to being used by the Ivans. Well. Some ladies are just romantic, aren't they?'

—

In the pre-dawn twilight, we saw that the way out of the valley was a narrow slope, between boulders and frozen streams which glinted like steel. At least we could see the way now, and there were no collisions and no delays from bunching up as we progressed, with the Hanomags positioned in the middle between the Tigers, up onto the steppe to rejoin the road heading west. The land up there was shrouded in a freezing, grey fog which suited our purposes well that day – and we prayed it would last long enough to keep us hidden from the air above and the horizons beyond.

The first thing we encountered, as we straddled the wider road and increased speed to twenty kph, was the wreckage of one of our columns that must have been hit the previous day, around the time that we were fighting our battle against the Stalins. The road here was littered with the wreckage of trucks and wagons, evidently hit from the air by the Sturmoviks or similar aircraft. In the fog, three big Opel lorries loomed up, lying on their sides, still smouldering, their drivers dead in the cabs in grisly, frozen contortions.

Steppe birds resembling inland gulls were roosting on the debris, and picking at the corpses. Horse-drawn carts were here too – smashed open by bombs, with the horses stiff and dead, their legs pointing skyward. One horse was still alive, quivering and kicking on the ice – but none of us could spare a precious bullet to put it out of its agony.

Dead men lay along the road also. In places, the explosions and fires had melted the ice, and the bodies had sunk into it, and now hands, arms and legs projected up from the glassy drifts into the mist along the roadside. One cart had been carrying provisions, and one of the Hanomags paused to scoop up the boxes of tins and packets from the mud.

This attack had not been entirely one-sided, however: in the steppe beyond the road, we could just make out a recently-crashed Russian Sturmovik, buried nose-down in the tundra, the red star on its tailfin glowing bright in the milky vapour. A few kilometres further on, we found out how it was shot down.

A Flak half-track was by the roadside, half in a ditch. Its qua-druple 20mm anti-aircraft cannon appeared undamaged, and as we approached, two young crew men emerged from the cab and waved to us frantically.

I slowed the Tiger to a halt so that Helmann could shout down to them from the turret cupola.

'What do you know of the Red positions?' he yelled.

'I believe they're close, Herr Ober,' one of the lads called up. The two of them looked like ragged schoolboys in their caps, mit-tens and greatcoats, with ice on their noses and their pinched cheeks. 'But we have no radio, no phone line. We shot a Red plane down,' he added proudly.

'I saw that, and I congratulate you. Does your Flak work?'

'If we can get it out of the ditch, sir, she'll work fine. We have fuel for another day or so.'

We hauled the Flak half-track onto the road until it spluttered into life, and it took up position behind the Hanomags. Good Flak cover was a lucky find, and these boys seemed to know their busi-ness. I wasn't sure how much they would need to do, though, as the fog seemed to cover us overhead, and even to left and right visibility was down to a hundred metres at most.

'Excellent retreating weather!' Kurt yelled at me over the bulk-head. 'We'll be at the river soon. And Helmann,' he added in a lower voice, 'Helmann will get some oak leaves on that pretty Iron Cross of his.'

'You think so?' Without my glass vision block, my face was frozen in the stream of air coming in, despite the balaclava and goggles I was wearing. 'Why?'

'Can't you see? He's got his own little battle group now, with his own Flak and everything. He even has a liaison officer from the Luftwaffe in the turret. In the Berlin Evening Post, they'll call us *Kampfgruppe Helmann, saviours of the eastern front.* He gets his *Kampfgruppe* back to the river, he defends the crossing and he safe-guards the whole front from a collapse. Into the bargain, he brings back an ultra-high quality prisoner with knowledge of codes and cyphers and *scheisse* knows what else, which makes a giant contribution to our military intelligence. It couldn't be better, could it?'

'You think that woman knows about cyphers and stuff?'

'I think she knows a lot more than she's saying. And Helmann thinks so, too. My God, but those interrogators will go to work on her with some energy. Such a pretty thing, too.'

I thought of her profile in the freezing dark, and the sudden scent of her hair. And then –

'*Scheisse*,' Wilf muttered. 'What is *that?*'

We were entering a forested area, and beside the road, a large tree spread its bare branches over us in the fog. Hanging from the bough, I saw a series of bodies – six in all – hanging by nooses from their necks, utterly still. We passed under them, and then under another three of them further along. The bodies were recently hanged, all male, and in Russian combat clothing of quilted jackets and felt boots.

'Those are partisans,' Helmann's voice came through the intercom. 'Better to have them up there than in the forests around us. Our troops have cleaned out this zone, evidently. And there's no time for reconnaissance now, we'll go straight into the forest.'

The hanging bodies rotated slightly as the hot air of our exhausts brushed underneath them as we advanced, while their staring eyes looked down at us from broken-necked heads.

'Partisans, this close to the river?' I said to Kurt.

'It looks like our boys dealt with them on the way through,' he laughed. 'See, there's another tree-load.'

The road became a narrow track through the forest, with trees close to us, many of their branches strung with these dangling bodies. The fog was thinner among the trees, and I could see great shadows in the forest depths that might have hidden anything. Our convoy began to slow and bunch up, and Helmann cursed the loss of momentum, giving orders from his cupola to get the route cleared.

One of the Hanomags pulled aside, belching oily smoke, and the crew began to dismount, seeking to attend to the engine. I caught sight of the woman prisoner in the back of the vehicle, still in her hunched pose, still with two troops watching her. The two nurses were in there too, reclining and looking rather weary after their exertions. Helmann was shouting questions to the Hanomag crew, when there was a flash of light from the track up ahead.

It was a red-orange light that flickered wildly, lighting up the trees, and then died away. Smoke came drifting back down the path, and the three remaining Hanomags all pulled off the road, their crews manning the cab machine guns. I drove forward into the vacated roadway, and advanced up the track, with Kurt hunched over his gun in readiness and Helmann barking questions into his radio to the other crews.

The panzer slithered around an angle in the track – and I saw the nearest Tiger on fire.

'An engine fire?' I said – but this was more than that.

The whole back of the Tiger was burning, with blazing liquid dripping down the hull and pooling in the road. A crewman was crouching on the turret, spraying an extinguisher – but as he laboured, I saw his head jerk back, and his skull fragmented into several pieces which span away in the misty air. His body flopped forwards, and landed in the pool of burning gasoline on the ground.

'*Scheisse*! Sniper!' Kurt said.

I heard Helmann come crashing back down into the turret; the gun traversed, and the hull echoed as Wilf the gunner sent a burst of his co-axial MG into the trees, shattering the frozen branches.

On the forest track, the crew in the burning Tiger had a choice – stay and fry in their machine, or take the chance in the open. They flew out of the hatches like rabbits, leaping down and sprinting for cover towards our Tiger. Puffs of mud flew up from the track as the sniper followed them with bullets, and one crew man was hit in the leg. As he lay, clutching his thigh, he was hit again in his torso, making his body convulse as the bullets ripped him up. One of his comrades began to run back to him, and that man was cut down as well, with a bullet going clean through his chest and ricocheting off our front plate. A Hanomag came careering past us, its gunner blasting his MG42 along the tree line, the twenty bullets per second demolishing entire trees in splinters of wood and ice.

Just as the Hanomag passed the dead men in the road, the flames came again.

'It's a flamethrower,' Kurt said, and he began shooting with his ball-mounted MG.

From the side of the forest track, a long line of flames was erupting – literally spurting from the shadows, and covering the Hanomag in front of us in a shower of orange flames. I saw the Panzergrenadier on the Hanomag MG drenched in this fire, his whole torso becoming a torch as it covered him, and then the flames splashed down into the open compartment. The rear doors opened, and two men tore out, their clothing on fire, followed by many other men completely engulfed in flames. They sprawled in the mud and ice, trying to beat the flames out, writhing and tearing at the ground.

Kurt was shooting MG rounds past the burning vehicle, hitting trees and bracken along the track, but I couldn't see his target, only a trail of burning liquid leading into the forest. We were in a bad situation – hemmed in by trees, facing woods full of shadows, the track clogged with slowed or stationary vehicles.

'He's by the fallen tree,' Helmann said in my ear. 'I see his flame. He's behind the fallen tree.'

There *was* a fallen tree in the shadows – a gnarled old thing, covered in ice. I saw the ice glimmer, reflecting the small flame that burns in a flame-gun nozzle and lights the jet of fuel. When close to a tank, a flamethrower can destroy a sixty-tonne monster in seconds, by burning out the grilles, sending liquid fire through the hatch seals – or blinding a driver who has no glass block to shield his face…

The 88mm roared above me, and the fallen tree blew up with a high-explosive round that lifted and threw it down many metres away. To no avail – the spurt of fire came again and poured across the road towards our Tiger, drenching the burning men in front of us in more flames. Both their Hanomag and the other Tiger were

fully ablaze now – the Hanomag with its dead MG gunner still standing at his gun, wreathed in smoke, and the Tiger with its crewman
in the pool of burning liquid in the road. The smell of burning
flesh came to me through the open vision port: a sickly, roasting
smell over the stench of gasoline.

Kurt kept firing, but the flamethrower shot out its tongue again,
splashing our drive wheel and coating our track-guards in a thick,
orange fire. One more burst like that, and we would be on fire
like our comrades. I reversed, but immediately we crashed into an
obstacle at the rear. Helmann shouted that this was another Tiger,
that we just reversed into our fellow panzer – and with that, I knew
there was a danger that two of us panzers would be trapped and set
ablaze by this one flame-gunner in the woods.

I shunted into forward gear, and took the Tiger forward so
quickly that the front lifted up off the ground; then I slammed the
hull down into the woods, sending trees flying out from under our
tracks. Kurt kept firing – and I could actually see the flame-gunner
now: a tall man hunched over a rifle-shaped weapon that was drib-
bling burning liquid, connected by a tube to a fuel pack on his
back. He was staggering as trees fell around him. He straightened
up and aimed at us, but Kurt was quick on his MG34.

Kurt's tracer rounds went right through the flame-gunner, piercing his fuel tank and sending plumes of fire out behind him as the
bullets tore through and went off into the woods. In his shadowy
hiding place, the man was suddenly lit up with flames – an absolute
spiral of fire that reached twenty or thirty metres into the air above
him. He slumped and disappeared in the blaze, while I reversed
back onto the path, dragging a couple of trees with us in the wheels,
and took up a position on the other side.

From there, I could see the chaos.

The Tiger that we had reversed into was stalled across the track,
blocking it, while in front of it the burning vehicles were both
engulfed in flames, the men on the ground burning as fiercely as
the machines they had jumped from. Ahead of that, a Tiger was
standing guard a few hundred metres away, its turret revolving

slowly, firing occasional bursts of MG into the trees. Our new Flak half-track was there, too, its barrels horizontal, traversing along the tree line and sending out bursts of thick, white tracer that smashed whole tree trunks to pieces.

'The Hanomags,' Helmann said. 'The verdamm prisoner. Get us back to the Hanomags, Faust.'

I drove directly into the trees, bulldozing several of them down with our hull front to force a path past the stranded Tiger. Roots and trunks whirled in front of us as we demolished a line of birches, and then we were back onto the track and heading back to the Hanomag group. I saw at once that a fight was happening there.

One of the Tigers that remained with the half-tracks was under attack from a ragged gang of partisans, who were crawling onto its hull, armed with bottles and grenades. The panzer was immobile, with one track shed loose along its hull, and although it was firing its MGs, this was doing nothing against the marauding anti-tank fighters. The other Tiger was reversing away, wisely keeping its distance, firing MG onto its comrade panzer to try to knock off the attackers. The Panzergrenadiers were out of their Hanomag transports, fighting hand to hand with other knots of Ivans, who were emerging from the trees with rifles, machine pistols and hand-held bombs.

The fighting was vicious – it was murderous, with men who had zero to lose using all they had against their enemies. One Grenadier, obviously out of ammunition, was slashing and stabbing at the Russians, his bayonet fixed, hacking at the partisans in the body and neck. Another was throwing aside his MP40 and seizing an entrenching spade, using that to beat back the men who charged at him. He was cut almost in half by a burst of heavy MG fire, which sent his guts spinning out across the ice, steaming in the frozen air. I saw a Russian close to our front as we halted, who threw a grenade onto our turret top which deflected off and exploded in the ditch. Kurt demolished the man with a few shots of his MG, and we came to a standstill with our tracks on top of his body.

The Hanomag with the Russian woman inside was directly opposite us.

'My prisoner,' Helmann said. 'I have plans for that *verdamm* prisoner. My God, and the nurses too, and the wounded. They're in that Hanomag.'

Wilf was hunched on his gun, sighting left and right, but –

'They're all too close,' he said. 'I'll hit our men in all this.'

Helmann cursed, and I saw pale light flood in as he opened the cupola.

'Faust, come with me,' he ordered.

I swallowed, took my MP40 from its holder on the hull wall, and opened my hatch.

The icy air filled my lungs, and the danger made me suddenly aware of the cold, the sounds and the flashes of light, my senses working hard to keep me informed. Helmann was already sprinting across the road to the nurses' Hanomag, which was surrounded by partisans; they were firing into its steel plate and smashing open the rear doors with rifle butts.

The surviving Panzergrenadiers were caught up in their own melee, trying to force back another gang of attackers from beyond the road. One of our troops was an inspiration to the rest – standing bareheaded in the face of the partisans' fire, shooting his MP40 into the trees as the attackers charged from the shadows. It took three partisans to bring him down with shots and blows, one Ivan wielding a Cossack sabre which decapitated the German and sprayed his blood in a great arc. The curve of blood shone briefly through the ice crystals hanging in the air, before fading away to mere vapour.

His comrades took up the cry, and began to drive the marauders into the trees, sending them tumbling back with shots and bayonet thrusts. There were still dozens, there were scores of partisans in the shadows among the trees.

I thought, My God – how many are there? It felt that half of Russia was venting their anger on us, tearing and clawing at us for every bad thing that we had done to them and their huge, empty country.

I looked away from the grim sight, and saw the partisans already inside the Hanomag where the nurses, the wounded and the Russian woman were stationed. Screams came from within, long female screams and shrieks in German. Helmann fired his MP40 into the swarm of partisans around the rear doors, and I shot down two of these as they dodged and tried to rush at us with machine pistols. The partisans scattered, but shots came from inside the half-track, made hollow by the enclosed steel walls, and we rushed up to the doors.

Inside there, I saw the wounded men, sprawled where they had tumbled on the benches and the floor. They had all been shot. The two nurses were also on the floor, their heads blown open and their blood pouring across the metal. The Russian prisoner woman was scrabbling in the blood on the floor. A huge Ivan fighter was standing over her, holding a machine pistol. She was holding a Walther pistol, which I guessed was the nurses' suicide pistol, and she was pointing it up at the partisan.

I raised my gun – but Helmann put a hand out and pushed my barrel down. He had a wicked, feline smile on his face, as he watched to see what would happen, even while the infantry fighting continued around us.

The partisan said something to the woman in Russian, and the woman shook her head. The partisan raised his machine pistol. Helmann raised his gun to preserve his prisoner – but the Russian woman saved herself. She shot the Ivan through the chest and stomach, three times in all, each bullet punching out of his back in a burst of steaming bone and flesh. She rolled out of the way as he toppled forward, his bulk practically obliterating the two dead nurses under him.

She looked at Helmann, then at me. She threw aside the nurses' pistol, and cursed us long and hard in Russian.

All along the track, the firing was dying down as the partisans withdrew. My Tiger sent the last of them on their way with a series of high-explosive shells that ripped open the treeline and churned the fog into spirals in the blast wave.

Helmann fired off his magazine at some figures disappearing into the darkness of the trees beyond the smoke. Then he put his MP40 up on one shoulder, lit a cigarette, and surveyed the scene.

'We have to get out of the forest,' he said. 'All this smoke will rise through the fog and show our location.'

I dragged my eyes away from the dead wounded, the two dead nurses and the partisan, and the desperate figure of the Russian woman as she clenched her fists and tried to stop herself weeping.

'The Reds killed the wounded,' I said, trying to make sense of the carnage in the half-track. 'And the nurses shot themselves, Herr Ober, as they said they would. They shot themselves rather than be raped by the partisans.'

'But not the Russian woman,' Helmann said. '*She* shot the Russian, rather than be raped. Put her in the Tiger. I want her with me.'

'Sir.'

—

We threw our dead, the ones not already burning, onto the hull of the blazing Tiger as it burned out of control, preferring them to be consumed by flames than by the animals of the Red forest. With heavy hearts, we blew up the Tiger that shed its track, unable to effect repairs in our urgency. With six Tigers now, plus three Hanomags and the Flak wagon, we formed up and drove out of the forest in the fog. The last thing I saw of our battleground was that Hanomag still burning, its MG42 gunner still alight at his gun, stripped to bone by the flames.

Further up the track, the Flak gunner boys had done a good job; they had seen a group of twenty partisans outflanking our column in the trees, and shot them to pieces with their quadruple cannons. The Russians' bodies were lying dismembered among the frozen roots of the woods, their corpses utterly shredded by the 20mm shells. The two young gunners were vomiting in the ditch.

We paused as they moved their Flak wagon into the convoy behind us.

Suddenly, I heard Helmann shout a warning from the cupola, and he loosed off a long burst of his MP40. I saw bits of tree branches fall to the ground. I expected another battle with a sniper, but I heard only Helmann, laughing in his *unheimlich* manner.

'Look up there, in the trees on the left,' he yelled.

I squinted up through the hatch.

'*Scheisse*,' Kurt said. 'Is that someone's head?'

Lodged in the fork of two branches above the track was a severed human head, pale and staring, looking straight down at us.

'I thought it was another sniper,' Helmann laughed. 'But it's just a partisan who was caught in the Flak cannon. See how high his head flew off? That must be ten metres at least. Move on, Faust.'

—

The situation in our panzer was unusual. The Russian woman was located behind me, sitting on the hull floor, leaning against the half-empty ammunition racks. The Luftwaffe pilot – who had performed well in his new role as loader – was detailed to watch her through the remaining journey. He put his pistol in his belt like a cowboy, and he evidently enjoyed his work, looking down at her from the turret.

I drove. I could feel the machine protesting at its beating, the running gear demanding adjustment and tightening, and the transmission calling for a transfusion of oil. None was available, and the Tiger moaned and cursed as the forest road petered out to nothing, and we emerged from the trees into a region of valleys and ravines which every panzer driver surveyed with a scowl.

Such a landscape was fatal to our vehicles. The Hanomags, maybe, could make it, with their light pressure and truck steering. But to ask a Tiger, already beaten up by action and Russian roads, to cover another fifty kilometres over boulders and ridges? We would be stranded, and become carrion for the Russian crows.

We halted, while Helmann studied his map.

In a minute, Helmann spoke to the panzer commanders over the radio, and in turn they shouted his orders down to the Hanomags and the Flak wagon.

'There's a road on the map,' he said. 'We will get on it and we won't stop. Hanomags, Tigers, everyone. We will protect each other, but nobody will stop. Most of us will get to the river and fight in its defence. Those that do, will be heroes there. Those that do not, will be heroes on the way. Questions?'

One of the Tiger commanders said, 'Herr Ober, where is the road?'

The road led across a high plateau to the north of the valleys, an old east-west route which our armies had used in 1941 and found manageable. It was wide and flat, and would be littered now with the debris of retreat, but what other option was there?

The fog was thinning out now, and the sun was dimly visible in the south. It was around midday, and slats of light came through jagged rips in the clouds, sending purple and bronze light across the landscape. We saw the road in the distance, a dark channel through the tundra, gleaming with ice and frost, pointing directly west to our salvation.

We halted for a few minutes, to prepare ourselves for this race to the river.

Kurt put a jinx on himself, I think, as I completed the last of my checks along the running gear, surrounded by exhaust smoke and the swirls of evaporating fog. The sun was suddenly bright, and showed up every crease on Kurt's face as he squatted on the hull top, listening to his headphones.

'Will the old cow make it?' he said.

I looked at the slackened track length, the worn link pins and the distortion to the drive wheel that had resulted from our crashing into trees in the forest – and then from reversing into our fellow Tiger.

'Ja, ja,' I said. 'She'll make it.'

'She won't, will she?'

'I'll point her west, go full speed, and she won't stop till Paris. We'll have a beer at the Eiffel tower, you and me.'

Kurt rubbed his craggy chin.

'I have this feeling that the panzer will make it, and you'll make it. But me, I won't make it.'

'Sure you'll make it. Why not?' I said.

Helmann shouted to us to board and start up.

'Why not?' Kurt said, lowering into his seat. 'It's the girl. She's bad luck.'

The Russian woman was on the hull floor behind us. From somewhere, Helmann had found a length of steel chain, and her wrists were now chained to the ammunition rack.

'She's not bad luck,' I said. 'She's ok.'

'What happened to all her Russian comrades, eh? And the crew of her Hanomag. And even the nurses with her. They all died. Isn't that bad luck?'

I didn't answer, but I started us off in the vanguard of the column, ploughing through the frozen steppe towards the road to our salvation. Helmann gave us a speech on the intercom, which also went out to the crews of the other Tigers…

'We came to this country to build a defence against Bolshevism and the ways of the Slav. My information from Divisional command is that this defence will now be decided on the river to the west. If the Reds cross that line, they will be in the heart of our eastern lands, and we have seen already today the destruction and rape that they will bring. We are a *Kessel* now, a roving cauldron of defiance. To the river!'

Kurt looked at me and winked, making 'iron cross' gestures at his throat.

—

The Sturmoviks found us almost as soon as the fog cleared.

They attacked from the west, to one side, so I saw them break through the grey clouds against a steel-blue sky. The fog had given way to a pale sun that stood over us as big as a moon, and was no more painful to look at. The planes were six in number; they left long vapour lines as they swooped down, and when their cannon started shooting, I saw their orange tracer ploughing across the steppe towards us.

Our Tiger was now in the rear of the convoy, and up ahead I saw the Flak wagon elevate and rotate its four 20mm cannon onto the Russian aircraft. With the connected thinking that comes from exhaustion and fear, I speculated whether those Flak boys would halt to give themselves a stable firing platform, or keep moving to stay with the column. They kept moving, meaning that they had the task of hitting mobile targets from a travelling platform, but at least their fire remained close to us, and we did not leave them behind on the plateau.

The Red planes came down in two waves of three. Their cannon fire was wild, sweeping over the barren landscape, knocking chunks of earth into the air.

The Flak lads fired, their bright, white tracer spiralling up, wide at first, but then with an astute correction they laid their line of fire in front of the descending planes. One of the Sturmoviks was pierced through the tailplane, which flew to pieces behind the aircraft, making it plummet into the ground and explode.

The other two Ivans dropped their bombs low, and the dart-shaped objects shot forwards through the air. Most of them struck wide in plumes of soil and ice, but one came screaming horizontally into the centre of our column, hitting a Tiger squarely in the side of the hull. I saw the explosion tear the wheels and track off, and the great panzer, travelling at forty kph, lifted onto its side in its momentum, trailing its loose track behind it. The Tiger rolled over onto its turret and slid along the tundra, upside down, until it hit a boulder and came to rest against that. There was a flash from under the engine bay, and coils of smoke rose into the blue-grey sky.

Nobody stopped, of course.

The Flak wagon kept firing, swivelling around to hit the second wave of planes, which were so low that their red stars loomed over us as we drove on. The Red cannon fire was more accurate from these pilots, and tore sideways into one of the Hanomags. The half-track was directly ahead of me, and I saw the shells go into the left of the Hanomag body and exit from the right, sending bits of steel spinning up into the air. Some shells appeared to be deflecting around inside the compartment, because the tracer came leaping out of the open top, carrying with it pieces of bodies and clothing. The rear doors of the Hanomag fell open – and the interior was full of smoke and sparks, with men tumbling over each other as they were shot to pieces.

Some men crashed from the open doors – and although I swerved, I could not avoid hitting two or three of them with my tracks while they were still rolling over on the ground. Those Panzergrenadiers who remained inside were lit up by an orange ball of flame as the fuel tank exploded, and the whole vehicle span around on its axis, throwing out burning men and burning equipment.

Our quick-thinking Flak gunners caught another Sturmovik in its web of tracer, but the shells deflected from its armoured belly in a shower of sparks. Truly, that thing was a flying panzer. Only when the tracer hit the propeller was the machine brought down, with the propeller blades disintegrating and whirling across the plateau. The plane itself rolled over on its back in the air, out of control, and its final act, by accident or malice, was to hurl itself into our leading Tiger.

The plane exploded against the panzer from the side – and the plane and the vehicle were hidden in a fireball that rose for hundreds of metres into the air. The Tiger kept moving, its momentum simply unstoppable, trailing a pillar of flames behind it as it careered away from the convoy. I saw the engine grilles fly off, and then the tracks, and finally the whole panzer impacted into a depression in the ground, its dish wheels scattered around it in flames. Only the huge 88mm barrel remained visible, pointing defiantly at the Russian skies.

The bombs of these planes knocked out another Hanomag, which disintegrated in a single flash and disappeared from view. A Tiger was hit on the turret, which was separated from the hull and sent spinning into the air behind it. The three crew were still in the turret cage, their bodies outlined by flames as they twisted. The hull threw out exploding ammunition as it continued to roll, with tracer rounds flying out in spirals of smoke.

The Red Sturmoviks returned for one final strafing run, and sent a furious stream of tracer all along our column. I heard shells strike our turret roof, with hammer blows and the screech of ricochets. I heard the Luftwaffe man begin praying fervently. Kurt fired his ball MG up at the planes as they raced away east, until his gun rattled empty.

Although we were still travelling at full speed, I glanced around to look at the Russian woman chained to the turret ring. She was laughing silently, looking up either at the Luftwaffe pilot, or beyond him to the Red pilots soaring away from us. She looked at me, and her green eyes were flecked with a kind of frenzy. I looked back out of my vision port, and kept driving.

We had one Hanomag left now, with four Tigers and the Flak wagon. The Hanomag was listing to one side, and its machine gun shield was shot away. The Tigers were trailing oily smoke, and the one ahead of me had a loose track which was buckling as it moved. My own Tiger was groaning as it moved, the running gear grinding as the dish wheels made friction against each other. On my dials, the oil pressure was red and the volt meter was at zero – I gave up looking at them.

'Thirty kilometres,' Helmann said in my headphones. 'We keep going. Nobody stops.'

Over the bulkhead, Kurt was reloading his MG34 with a new magazine drum.

'My last one,' he said, kissing it. 'My special baby. I filled it with the special rounds – the hollow-nosed ones. Any Ivan who gets between me and that river gets this.'

'We get to the river – and then what?' I said.

'Then the next river, and the next one, and the river after that.'
'All the rivers, back to the Reich?'
He didn't answer me, as he fitted the magazine.

—

Two Tigers in front, then the two half-tracks, then our third Tiger and finally us. We had to slow because the road was cratered and strewn with boulders, and the change in speed only demonstrated how much maintenance the Tiger needed. The transmission was steaming with oil, and the compartment was filled with acrid fumes that made me glad of the cold air blasting in through my open visor.

The road became crowded with retreating troops.

We passed knots of infantry, slogging their way west without officers or transport. They tried to flag us down, but we kept going, following the wide, rough road towards the river. We passed wagons, mobile kitchens and radio trucks, towed artillery and troops on horseback, all the flotsam of a full-scale retreat, and everyone heading for the safe barrier of the river.

The only gauge that I looked at now was the fuel dial – and that was touching zero. The Tiger drank three litres of gasoline to cover each kilometre, even at optimum speed. At high speed, and with all the revving and manoeuvring we had done in the forest, we were consuming five or even six litres per kilometre. I alerted Helmann to this, and he cursed. He jumped down, and appeared crouching behind me in the hull, banging his fist on the bulkhead gauges.

'They've been wrong before,' he said. His breath was thick with cognac.

'Not the fuel gauge, Herr Ober. The fuel is accurate.'

'Verdamm gasoline will lose us this war. Those Reds are lucky, they can burn as much diesel oil as they like; they get it from the Caucasus.'

'What shall I do, sir?'

He slammed the bulkhead.

'How many more kilometres left?'

'Five, maybe six. It's operating on fumes, sir.'

'We will take fuel from another vehicle. Stop when I tell you.'

'Sir.'

I thought that he meant to transfer fuel from one of the other Tigers – but of course they were running as low as we were. The huge disc of the sun had whitened and faded into the sky, and the air now was gunmetal-coloured, and sparkling with crystals of ice. To run out of fuel here, on the open plateau, almost within sight of the river – that would be a cruel fate, leaving us to hobble the last few kilometres on foot, pursued by Ivan.

'There,' Helmann said, slapping my shoulder as he hunched behind me, and pointing through the vision slit. 'See those truck transports. We'll take fuel from them. You, radio man, radio the other Tigers.' Helmann clambered back up into the turret.

'I don't think he remembers my name,' Kurt said as we halted.

I thought that was probably true.

—

The trucks were in a convoy of about ten: big Deutz lorries churning and slipping through the ice, making a stately five or six kph. As soon as we came alongside, they knew what we wanted. We pushed our Tigers close to them, forcing them to slow down and stop. One by one, they ground to a halt, and our three Tigers and two half-tracks came to a stop likewise. I cut the engine and climbed up through the hatch to see what was what. From the leading truck, a man in a civilian fur coat was standing on the running board, shouting at Helmann. His officer's cap had the skull insignia of the SS.

'Get away from my vehicles,' he was yelling. 'I am on the business of the Schutz Staffel and these are our transports.'

'What is in your trucks?' Helmann called down from the cupola.

'That is not your concern. Move your panzers and let us proceed.'

'My panzers are needed for the defence of the river. We must have fuel.'

'You will take no fuel from us,' the SS officer shouted. 'You will be shot for this.'

I heard Helmann cackle with laughter. I noticed a few snow-flakes drifting in the air, glinting in the overcast light, as hard as wire. The SS man reached into his cab and brought out a Luger machine pistol - an effeminate little gun that the police and security troops used. Helmann roared with laughter – and I was glad that I didn't have to smell his breath.

We were saved from the confrontation by the Red Army itself.

One of the Deutz wagons was lifted off its wheels, and its metal sides split apart. A tracer round came out of the side, shooting across the road and disappearing across the plateau. The next round that hit was high explosive, and this blew the truck's roof and walls off, sending them rotating in the falling snow. From inside the truck's load compartment, thousands of small white shapes emerged, drift-ing in the air. Small, tubular shapes which I realised were –

'Smokes,' Kurt said. '*Scheisse* cigarettes.'

Our turret was already traversing left to aim at the attackers.

'Face left, driver,' Helmann shouted. 'T34s.'

I rotated left, crunching our hull front against the nearest Opel truck and ripping its side open. Bottles fell out – bottles of wine, it appeared, which broke and splattered red on our prow. The smell of booze came in through the vision slit. I pushed forward to get past the truck, bulldozing it aside in a flurry of breaking glass and red wine. When we were clear, I saw the T34s on the plateau, through the snowflakes. Three of them. They were racing – faster than I ever saw a tank move before – perhaps proud of their chance to trap a panzer before the main army caught up behind them. They moved light and stripped down – their hulls bare, unpainted metal and their tracks throwing out streams of ice as they flattened down and charged at us across the steppe.

The 88mm gun over my head boomed out, and in the echo I heard the Russian woman in the hull behind me wailing. I looked round at her, and saw the empty shell case from the gun breech crash down on her, smoking with cordite. She convulsed and kicked it away like a rat.

Four Tigers against three T34s. This should have been an easy battle, but something in the way those Ivan tanks charged – the way they spat flames from their exhausts and ripped up the tundra below their tracks – that told me these crews weren't interested in odds or calculations. They wanted to get a Tiger.

One of them, in the lead, was hit by a round from the Tiger on our right. I saw the shell smash into the turret and knock a scab of metal off, in a burst of debris. The T34 kept charging – in fact, it accelerated, with the air behind it distorting in its exhaust heat and the snow flying around it in a slipstream. It was hit again, on the hull front, and this round smashed off the driver's visor, which span away.

The machine kept charging – so quickly that our gunners were shooting past it as it ploughed under their elevation, the 88mm rounds smacking into the fallen snow in useless puffs of white. A hundred metres from us, it began firing, and a round hit our gun mantle with a scream, deflecting down into the ground to bury itself. Our Luftwaffe friend began babbling his devotions again, and, over all the noise, the cursing and shooting, I heard the Russian woman laughing.

We shot straight into the hull front, and I saw our round penetrate and the T34's structure shudder as the projectile whirled around inside there. By now I could see the face of their driver, in his smashed-open vision slit, a face covered with blood and neither dead nor alive. I saw that he was Asiatic, perhaps a Mongolian, with almond-shaped eyes and a goatee beard. That was the last thing I saw before he crashed his doomed tank into our line.

The T34 smashed through one of the Deutz lorries, and embedded itself into one of our Tigers, making the huge panzer rock sideways. I saw the SS commander in his fur coat jump from his wagon and run, as the Tiger began to reverse away from the impacted T34. The panzer lurched backwards, slithered in the roadway, and knocked down the SS man bodily. The Tiger crew had no idea of this, of course, and kept reversing. The SS man's body was dragged up onto the tracks, the handsome fur coat torn to shreds, and then thrown out at the front.

The other two T34s charged right past us, lifting off the ground completely as they crossed the road, and literally flew off into the steppe on the other side.

The smashed T34 stood in the wreckage of the Deutz, its hatches opening up.

The two men who emerged were bloody, but I could see that their faces were lit by vengeance, battle-lust and perhaps vodka too. They jumped from the T34 just as a high-explosive 88mm round burst against it, showering them with fragments. An armour-piercing round went through the turret and erupted out of the open hatch like a rocket, heading skyward. By then, though, the two Red tank men were walking calmly towards our Tiger, holding pistols. Kurt, beside me, gripping his MG, laughed softly as he aimed.

Something reminded me of the previous tank battle – when those three Red infantry soldiers had appeared from that Stalin tank, looking for something. I glanced around at the Russian woman, and saw her staring through the vision slit, trying to see what was happening out there. I looked ahead again, just as Kurt opened fire with his special hollow-nosed bullets.

The effect of the hollow rounds on the two Ivans was catastrophic. Hit directly in their torsos, their arms were severed, and pieces of the exploding bullets flew out of their backs, trailing steam. One man was hit in the face, and his jawbone was smashed off, his teeth whirling like the snowflakes; the other man was hit in the belly, and his genitals were shot away as the slug did its work inside him and fragmented downward. The bodies lay steaming and smoking on the road, surrounded by pools of red SS wine and hundreds of cigarettes.

'Nice,' Kurt said.

'Turn this panzer around,' Helmann yelled in my earphone. 'Faust, wake up, damn you.'

I shook myself, and rotated the Tiger on its differential, smashing the big cargo lorry again, so that we faced the two T34s that had leaped sideways across our roadway. They were turning around also, having travelled hundreds of metres in their impetus, and were now spinning to face us head-on.

I remembered the blank, almond eyes of the other driver, and I knew these were Russians from the interior of the Soviet Union, men with no fear, no nerves, and no hesitation. They didn't care if they lived one minute and died the next, unlike us with our prayers and our politics. These were the men we were sent into Russia to fight, to keep them away from our culture and our architecture and our racial purity.

I must confess that I pissed myself.

Those T34s fired like maniacs, like lunatics, advancing on us through the snow that was now falling thickly out of the leaden sky behind them. Their bare steel hulls seemed to be part of the sky, part of the soil, part of Russia itself. Even when we shot their tracks off, they kept firing. Even when we blew the turret off one of them, the other kept advancing. Its shells struck us on the hull between Kurt and me, opening a crack of light between the vertical front and the hull roof over our heads, before the round ricocheted off. It raced to one side to hit us in the flank, but I rotated the Tiger onto it, feeling the Maybach engine falter as our fuel ran dry.

We shot that T34 in the turret, cracking it open like an egg and throwing the crew out across the steppe. We hit it in the hull, making the engine erupt in flames, and still the thing advanced on us. We shot though the front plate, splitting it open and making the whole thing spin around on its axis, trailing flames, coming to rest facing away from us.

The Tiger next to us put a round into its back plate.

The engine flew up out of the hull, dripping with burning oil, its pistons still cranking against the sky. Then the fuel ignited, and the T34 was enveloped in orange flames.

I wiped my face.

Beyond the burning T34, other vehicles were approaching us.

These were similar in appearance to T34s, but with no turret; the open hull ring filled with the heads and shoulders of soldiers in Red Army helmets. They were using these turretless tanks as personnel carriers, bringing soldiers into the conflict inside their sloped armour.

We shot up one of these things with an armour-piercing round, and the warhead caused obvious carnage inside the hull, as pieces of men and their weapons came flying out, on fire. That vehicle was hit again with high-explosive, and the whole machine tipped over, spilling its dozen occupants onto the ground and crushing them as a mother bear crushes its cubs. The other turretless tank still came on, however, taking two deflections off its front plate, until it came in below the elevation of our guns and slewed onto the road among us.

Our Flak wagon, which had remained silent all this time, now opened up, sending a hail of tracer down the road and onto the T34 soldier-carrier. The 20mm tracer shells rebounded off the sloped armour in a whirlwind of light, decapitating some of the soldiers inside who were still watching out of the turret ring. Their heads flew away across the road with the tracer that beheaded them. Our Flak paused, however, and I saw our Flak boys reloading the huge 20mm magazines one by one. The Tigers traversed and fired on the intruder, but by then the load of troops were scrambling out of the open hull, ten of them, and massing in the road. The T34 was blown apart behind them, but the Ivans didn't even flinch as pieces of the armour plate flew around them.

Our last remaining Hanomag, packed with Panzergrenadiers, came alive as its crew poured out into the combat.

Our men were ragged, scorched, low on ammunition, but armed with anything they could hold. Like furious scarecrows they tore into the bunched groups of fresh Russians in the road, and the two enemies clawed at each other for survival. I saw a Panzergrenadier hacking at the throat of a Russian with an axe from the Hanomag's tool kit, while his comrade used a pickaxe to pierce an Ivan's chest. The Reds reeled, then regained their spirit, and fired into the Grenadiers, pouring bullets into them. One German manned the MG in the Hanomag's cab, and shot down two of the Ivans before he was blown down by fire from the other Russians' guns.

Beside me in the Tiger, Kurt aimed his MG, paused, aimed again and paused. Always, the troops were too close together, fighting hand to hand, for him to fire on. Indeed, all our Tigers held their fire, their turrets traversing across the steppe, looking for more threats, while the infantry fought to the death in the road among us.

Whenever a Russian emerged from the carnage and approached a Tiger, he was shot immediately by a ball-mounted Tiger MG. If a Panzergrenadier tried to withdraw, he was cut down in a few paces by Russian fire. We in the Tigers saw our Grenadiers decimated, man by man, and the open road become a charnel house as the infantry slaughtered each other. In the end, three Russians remained standing, and they leaped over the German corpses to burst into the empty compartment of the Hanomag.

'Are you looking for something, Ivans?' Helmann muttered in my earphones. 'What are you seeking in there, my Red friends?'

Kurt fired on these three Ivans, and his hollow rounds spattered around them against the Hanomag sides – but the Russians were astute, and evidently accustomed to working under fire. One threw a grenade at us, and its blast blinded me for a moment, while Kurt held fire until he could see. By then, the Russians were swarming over the nearest Tiger, with grenades in their hands.

The MG men of the other panzers opened up, smacking the Tiger along its hull with MG rounds, and killing one of the Reds, who slumped into the road. The other two, though, ducked behind the Tiger's turret and disappeared. The Tiger began to rotate in the road, spinning on its axis point, trying to throw the men off its hull and crush them under the track links. It achieved this – and both men were hurled off as the panzer span around, their bodies being mangled beneath the treads. A moment later, though, their grenades exploded on the engine deck.

I saw the Tiger spin yet more frantically as its engine surged – and then shudder to a halt as it lost power. Dense smoke came from the engine grilles, and flames issued from the exhaust tubes – not the sparking flames of a Maybach running properly, but oily fire that showed the engine was now alight. The panzer rocked back and forth, then went still, as the flames grew higher, standing bright orange and black against the myriad glints of the falling snow.

'We have three Tigers now,' Kurt said, as we watched the panzer's deck burn, and the Tiger crew jumped clear of the flames from the hatches. 'A *Kampfgruppe* of three Tigers.'

'And a Flak,' I said. 'And we found some gasoline.'

Before that burning Tiger was completely engulfed in flames, I ran over to it, reached into the driver's hatch and took out the glass vision block – a great prize, which I fitted to my Tiger proudly.

—

We pumped fuel from the big Deutz lorries with hand cranks, working frantically as the snow thickened and built up on the steppe around us. Their fuel tanks were well filled. The truck drivers, all SS men, watched us viciously, with the mangled body of their officer, still in his fur coat, lying steaming on the snowy ground. We were driven by urgency. The snow might protect us from air attacks, but the main Red army could not be far away. Indeed, gangs of retreating men came running past us as we worked, shouting that the Reds were five kilometres distant, or three. A Kettenrad half-track came clattering past, a set of tracks with a motorbike wheel at the front, made for one man and now carrying four who clung on desperately.

I checked the fuel gauge, and saw that we had enough now for maybe thirty kilometres – enough to get to the river. The other two Tigers had the same, and we syphoned the fuel from the Hanomag and put it in the Flak wagon, which carried our dismounted crew men too. We replenished our small arms ammunition from the bodies in the roadway, and fired up the Tiger engines, ready to leave.

The road was strewn with dead Germans, dead Russians, pieces of debris from the smashed Deutz trucks, red wine and thousands of cigarettes, all sinking into the mud and being covered in snow. The last Deutz truck in the line was untouched, though, and as we were leaving, I couldn't resist seeing what was inside the thing. More black market goods, or was it something more useful? I nudged the truck's body with the front of our tracks as we went past, ripping a long hole in the flimsy metal sides, and tearing the truck open from end to end.

I stopped the panzer and stared inside.

The interior of the vehicle was fitted out like some kind of bar, or night club. It had velvet drapes on the walls, couches, a chandelier swaying in the ceiling, and a very large bed covered in furs and quilts. Seated on the couches, and sprawled on the beds, were several women – maybe half a dozen – in stylish underwear and night dresses, staring back at me with shadowed, bleary eyes. Most of the girls had bruises and cuts, and they all looked drunk. Drunk, drugged and apparently unaware of what was happening around them.

'I've heard about this, but I've never seen it,' Kurt said. 'It's an officers' mobile brothel. That would keep you warm on a cold night, eh?'

'Move on, Faust,' Helmann ordered me through the intercom. 'Follow the other panzers.'

We left the exposed brothel, its complement of drugged whores and the wreckage of the battle as we moved off and followed the outline of the road visible as a darker ribbon through the snow on either side.

'An officers' brothel. That's where *she'll* end up,' Kurt said, gesturing behind him to the hull and the Russian woman still chained to the turret ring. 'If there's anything left of her after the interrogators are finished. I've heard they have special ways to make Russian women talk.'

'She's just a radio operator.'

'Yeah? Did you see those Ivans in the T34s without the turrets? They came racing up here to look for something, just like those other three foot soldiers who appeared yesterday. I think they were looking for a certain missing radio team, and Helmann thinks so too. She'll be talking soon enough, anyway.'

I shrugged, although I too had heard stories about what our intelligence interrogators did to women, the methods they used and how quickly women talked in their presence. I tried not to think about them doing their work on the Russian woman behind me.

They used a table, I had heard, and pieces of steel tube.

I kept a fifty-metre distance between our Tiger and the two in front of us, the last three panzers remaining of our twenty-strong company from the previous day. The Flak wagon was scuttling along out in front of them, picking its way around the abandoned carts, cars and dumped equipment which we in the panzers could bull-doze aside or simply crush. The Tigers in front of me flattened a series of Kubelwagen cars abandoned in the axle-deep mud, and smashed aside a giant artillery gun on a ten-wheeled carriage that was tipped on its side across the road. The knots of straggling troops jumped out of our way, or implored us for a ride to the river point, but we stopped for nobody now.

I knew that even when we got to the river, our first task would be to immediately fight in defence of the crossing point, to hold back the reds as long as possible. The thought filled me with cold in my spirit.

'The river,' Helmann said at one point. 'It is beyond this ridge. Keep following the road.'

The road was becoming impossible to trace, however, from my driving position, even with my handsome new vision block in place. The path of differently-coloured snow was being wiped away, and the whole landscape in front of us was a single, uniform expanse of Russian snow.

'It'll be two metres deep by the morning,' Kurt muttered. 'Or three. It'll be a *schneeslacht* tomorrow, a snow battle for that bridge.'

Up ahead, the Flak wagon was struggling to make progress; I could see it on a curve, its tracks spinning and throwing out chunks of ice. The leading Tiger got behind it and pushed it clear, and with many operations like that our three panzers plus the Flak crawled and groaned over the crest of a ridge, and angled down onto the other side. There, through the dense snow, I could just make out the river in the middle distance.

The river, at last.

It was a wide, black band set between white banks, its surface reflecting the steely clouds overhead. I saw the crossing point immediately – and as we progressed slowly down the slope, I took a look at the crossing through my binoculars. I saw immediately why it was so vulnerable to Red attack, and why we had to defend it.

The bridge itself was a steel structure barely a hundred metres in length, and easy to blow up as our forces retreated. It stood, however, at a narrow point in the river, where the wide channel was compressed by outcrops of land on both sides. Even with the bridge blown, determined construction troops could surely throw another bridge across the narrow channel in hours. This would send the Red avengers hurtling onto the western bank and the borders of the Reich itself, which lay beyond the white, frozen horizon.

The slope of the high ground leading down to the river was a chaotic sprawl of vehicles, some moving and some abandoned. Two old Panzer IV types, with extra armour cladding on their turrets, were grinding their way down to the crossing. Red Cross medical trucks were making the same journey, and I pitied the shattered men inside as the vehicles lurched and bucked down the gradient. Hanomags and armoured cars slithered alongside lines of men with shouldered rifles, trudging ceaselessly downhill. The road was completely gone, and the troops and transports were spread out over a wide area, each traveller finding his own way down from the ridge to the river.

The crossing was guarded by two large concrete PAK bunkers, and a few dug-in Panther panzers with their very distinctive curved gun mantles, their long 75mm barrels pointing up at the steppe.

The bridge itself was a mass of vehicles and men, moving past and over each other, a living snake of men desperate to get across to the west before the Ivan pincers closed upon them. With my binoculars, I could see military field policemen in a few places along the bridge – the police with metal insignia on chains around their necks which gave their nickname of 'Chain Dogs.' They were trying to control the flux of retreating troops, and at times shots were fired in the air to make a point.

I saw a Hanomag on the bridge, a vehicle of the type we called 'The Walking Stuka,' fitted with rocket launchers on its hull; it lost control in the traffic and veered between the upright girders of the bridge span. It see-sawed for a second on the parapet. Then it toppled forward into the jet-black water, its tracks churning in a froth of spray, until it disappeared from sight. I saw nobody exit from its cab.

'Follow those Panzer IVs down the slope,' Helmann told me. 'Stay in their tracks. If they can make it, we can make it.'

The snow was thicker than ever now, and without my binoculars the river below us was just a blur of black against white. Our three Tigers, with the Flak in front, followed the general direction that the Panzer IVs had taken, although in effect the impression of their treads was rapidly erased by the fresh snowfall.

We passed a Chain Dog officer who had his MP40 placed against the head of a wrong-doer, kicking the man in the back as he drove him ahead down the incline. There were several bodies lying in the snow, which seemed to have been shot in summary executions, as they were in a neat line with their boots removed for some unknown reason, and arranged in front of them. Passing infantrymen seized on the boots to replace their own worn-out gear, and carried them away eagerly. Some wounded men sat or lay in the snow, mute, looking in a pleading way at the passing traffic.

'Shall I stop for the wounded, Herr Ober?' I asked Helmann on the intercom.

'No. They will be picked up. Keep driving.'

The journey down the slope took almost an hour, with pauses as the traffic around us bunched up and vehicles crossed each other's paths with shouted curses. I saw one man being run down by the Panzer IV ahead of us, his legs crushed but the man still alive, white-faced with shock as the panzer rolled away from him and a red stain spread across the snow around him. We had to barge a stalled Stug self-propelled gun out of our way, forcing it away into deeper snow while the crew yelled and threatened us from the hull roof. In the end, we came to the foot of the hill, and rolled up among the hundreds of troops who were thronging between the two concrete PAK bunkers and pouring on to the girder bridge itself.

'Who is in command here?' Helmann yelled at a soldier beside one bunker, manning an anti-aircraft MG post. The man saluted, and gestured down into the bunker, and then turned his greatcoat collar up against the cold.

———

I took my MP40 and accompanied Helmann into the bunker. The Russian woman was still on the hull floor, shivering and panting, although the air inside the Tiger was barely freezing compared to the conditions outside. The bunker itself was well-heated, with electric lights and the scent of a woodstove somewhere deep inside. The commander was a grey-haired artillery officer who studied us with bloodshot, dilated eyes.

'Yes?'

'I have brought three Tigers and a Flak for the defence of the crossing.'

'Excellent. You will please dig in the Tigers in conjunction with the Panthers that we have. I expect the Reds to attack us very soon. The front has collapsed and the situation is very changeable.'

'I have a high-value prisoner who must be taken to military intelligence.'

'Put him on a transport,' the officer shrugged. 'The Chain Dogs will be leaving us soon, they can take him.'

'It is a woman. She has important knowledge. I can only hand her to intelligence interrogators personally. She is significant, not just a normal prisoner. The Reds have already tried to recapture her from me.'

'Who is she – Stalin's favourite whore?'

'I believe she has information about radio encryption.'

The artillery man raised an eyebrow, but shrugged again.

'You are fighting with us here. You can keep your prisoner with you, or give her to the Chain Dogs. You make the decision, Herr Ober.'

In the concrete entrance at the bunker's rear, the daylight was fading, and the rattle of vehicles, the shouts and curses of men, the keening of the wind, all came from beyond a descending curtain of snow that blotted out the sight of the retreat.

I saw Helmann thinking it over. I guessed it was a difficult decision for him. He wanted to be associated with the capture of this prisoner, I could see that. Giving her to the military police would break his claim on her. But to keep her here as the Russians surrounded us?

'Shall we take her across the bridge, sir?' I asked.

'No,' he snapped. 'In all that chaos, she will be killed or she will escape, and her value will be lost. We keep her in the Tiger, and let's get ready.'

'Sir.'

When we got back into the Tiger, though – the woman was gone. Her chain dangled empty on the turret cage, and the Luftwaffe man was nowhere to be seen either. Wilf was asleep on the gunner's seat, and Kurt was snoring in the hull front. Helmann kicked Wilf awake.

'Where is the *verdamm* woman, man? And where is the *scheisse* pilot?'

Wilf had no idea. The snow fell on our panzer, turning it white.

—

We found the two of them in a drift of snow beside the Tigers. We heard the woman before we saw her – grunting and gasping, and we waded through the white powder into a pocket of snow away from the road by the river. There were several corpses here, who were wounded men that had been left to die alone, with bandages and splints still on them. There was also the Russian woman, on her back, and the Luftwaffe man in his muddy flying suit, on top of her, unbuttoning his crotch and getting his hand over the woman's mouth to silence her.

I locked eyes with her, over the pilot's shoulder, and saw she was fighting hard – that she would fight all of us if necessary, until her strength gave out. That was not necessary, of course. Helmann kicked the pilot in the head, then again in the arse, and the man rolled off the prisoner and thumped the snow in frustration.

'This is just some fun, Herr Ober,' he said.

'You know that this prisoner is important to me,' Helmann said calmly. 'I told my crew to keep her in the panzer. That means you.'

'She wanted a piss,' the pilot said, grinning. 'And she's a fine sight squatting in the snow.'

'Idiot,' Helmann muttered. 'Luftwaffe idiot. This prisoner could change the course of this campaign. The course of the war.'

'I think you are exaggerating, Herr Ober,' the pilot laughed. 'But I take it that I am discharged from your crew? You have spare men on the Flak wagon now. I can make my own way across the bridge and rejoin my *geschwader*.'

Helmann laughed in his unique way.

The woman stood up, panting and wiping her mouth, her chest heaving. The Luftwaffe pilot began to turn, and I thought he was going to run from us without further discussion. But then the sky over the river lit up in an orange flash, and a dreadful boom made my eardrums deaden. I saw pieces of debris whirling through the air over the river, illuminated by that huge orange flame, which was turning red and expanding as it burned. The four of us – me, Helmann, the pilot and the Russian woman – stood and stared at the fragments raining down onto the river, falling thicker and faster even than the snow. I realised that these were fragments of bodies – pieces of the men that had been crossing the bridge, now scattered to the air of Russia.

The explosions came rapidly, each one a ball of orange fire that lit up the whole river from our side to the other. Some of them hit the water, sending up clouds of steam, and some hit the bridge, turning it into a slaughterhouse. The four of us ran back to the

Tiger, Helmann dragging the woman by her elbow, and me pushing the pilot in front of us. The pilot jumped very willingly into the panzer, which certainly looked like the safest place to be at that moment, and I slid through my hatch into my driver's seat.

I felt the Russian woman behind me, looking over my shoulder through the vision slit, both of us watching the explosions outside.

'Katyushas,' Kurt muttered. 'The Stalin Organ. Those rockets fly for six or seven kilometres, and they can fire twenty in a minute.'

The rockets were crashing in from somewhere further down the river bank, somewhere to the south, leaving trails of fire in the curtain of snow. They were hitting the bridge in salvos of three or four now, sometimes bouncing off the girders and spinning away into the air, but at other times exploding right on the crossing.

The vehicles on the bridge were being blown off into the water below, dozens of Opel trucks and Kubelwagens crashing down into the sheer black current. Even a Panzer II reconnaissance tank was thrown sideways; its commander was silhouetted in the hatch, flailing his arms, as the machine plummeted vertically into the river. As for the foot soldiers, they were carved up by the blast waves and metal fragments, their limbs whipping around as the impacts tore through the mass of men trapped on the channel. I saw one man who had gone mad, ripping his uniform off and standing on one of the girder arms, shouting into the air as the rockets came over again.

A projectile hit the steel beam and raced along the bridge surface without exploding, scything down men left and right until it ricocheted right off the far side. Men climbed the girders, threw themselves from the bridge, shot each other in the cut-throat stampede to reach the far side before the next impact. The air was full of screaming, detonations and the howl of the Katyusha rockets. The snowfall slackened off, and in the drifting flakes, as the bombardment ceased, the extent of the mayhem on the bridge was obvious. Scores of burning, dismembered bodies lay there, together with burning vehicles and many horses, some dead and some alive.

One horse was on fire, kicking and bucking as its hide flickered with flames. It trampled many of the wounded men, its hoofs slamming into their bodies again and again, until someone shot it dead and it slumped, still burning, on the roadway.

The bridge structure was still intact. Its girders were torn and twisted, but the hundred metres of hard crossing were still in place. Realisation of this fact led to a renewed rush among the retreating infantry, with men charging onto the bridge before the next salvo fell.

'We'll have to go and find that Katyusha,' Helmann said. 'The Reds have smuggled it in somewhere close, under cover of the snow. It'll go silent now, and then it'll open up again overnight. If those rockets hit our few panzers, the Reds will storm across here in the morning.'

It was typical of him not to reflect on the casualties on the bridge, but to prioritise its defence as a strategic point.

'You mean to take the Tiger along the riverbank, Herr Ober?' I said. 'In the dark, the snow, with our low fuel?'

'Start the engine, Faust.'

—

We put the Russian girl into one of the other Tigers, and left them stationed near the bridge with the Panthers and the old Panzer IVs, their gun barrels traversing slowly.

The Luftwaffe pilot was still in place in our turret, functioning as our loader, which appeared to be Helmann's way of punishing him for interfering with the prisoner. The pilot had lost his arrogance, and was pale and chastened. It occurred to me that, despite being a Stuka pilot, he had never seen the effect of explosions on a packed group of men at first hand.

I drove the Tiger at walking pace up onto the riverbank, where there were open fields that had not been mined. Thank God I had taken that new glass block for my vision slit – but even so, I could see virtually nothing outside except drifting snowflakes and the light of fires from the bridge behind us. Helmann gave me directions from the cupola, and we kept up a steady advance, with the blank, dark space of the river on our right.

The rockets had come from somewhere down here, following the line of the river, but there were many small loops and dents in the riverbank where anything might be concealed in the snow and the dark.

We prowled around one such bay, unable to see anything. I kept an eye on the fuel gauge, making sure that we could had enough in reserve to get back to the bridge. We went on for several kilometres like this, with me hoping fervently that Helmann's famously sharp eyesight was good enough to pick out features in the landscape, and not send us crashing down the bank into the freezing water. The bank was fringed in places with tall, spindly rushes white with frost, and these formed screens around some of the bays and inlets. There could have been half the Red Army hiding in some of those places, and no German would have seen them until daylight.

Just as I told Helmann that we were reaching the limit of our fuel, he ordered me to steer 45 degrees, go twenty metres and then cut the engine. I did so, and the sudden quiet was broken by the clang of contracting steel in the engine bulkhead, and the moan of the wind over the hull. I could hear Helmann giving quiet, urgent commands to Wilf on the 88mm, and Kurt was hunched over his MG beside me, squinting out to try to see what was ahead. I could see only a screen of those frozen rushes, and some distant fires on the German-held side of the river.

'There,' Helmann said. 'A cigarette glow.'

He had good eyes. There *was* a glow, very faint, among the reeds, and in the slanting snowflakes, there was a dark outline in the river beyond.

'Fire a white flare,' Helmann ordered me.

The flare pistol was in a fire-proof box on the hull wall behind me. I primed it with the utmost care, because the effect of a mag-nesium flare shooting around in our compartment, spitting out flames, would be far worse than an MP 40 going off accidentally. I opened the hatch, aimed the pistol over the river, and fired.

'Holy *scheisse*,' Kurt said.

We all uttered something similar. The small flare exploded at about 200 metres height, and as it swayed down, its luminous glow showed up a large, raft-like boat in the rushes, fitted with machine guns on the bow and a rack of steel tubes on the hull, pointing directly downriver at the bridge.

The crew saw us as soon as we saw them, and they froze for a moment, in their Russian fur caps, quilted tunics and excellent felt boots. The crew was about a dozen men, engaged in the process of loading more Katyusha rockets onto the firing racks. The idiot who had been smoking on the bank was caught like a rabbit in head-lights, his ragged cigarette still in his mouth.

Behind him, the boat crew dropped the rockets and grabbed their guns, but Wilf and Kurt were firing their MGs into the boat, ripping steel plates out of its hull. A moment later, Wilf fired high-explosive, and the round hit the bow, sending the MG position fly-ing and dumping the rocket launcher tubes over on their sides.

Small arms fire smacked into our front plate as I started the engine and advanced a few metres towards the bank, with our 88mm firing two more rounds of shrapnel burst. The Red soldiers were thrown into the water, or flung onto the reeds along the bank, their bodies issuing smoke and flames. In the blast, a Katyusha rocket exploded, and then another – and in seconds the whole boat was gone, replaced by a faint outline on the water surface, full of flames. Its bow broke off and drifted away, trailing fire until it vanished into the falling snow.

'But how many more are there?' Helmann muttered.

'Our fuel is at minimum, sir,' I said.

He cursed. 'Then we will take a prisoner if one of these is alive. He will tell us their disposition. Hull gunner, go and see if there is a live one.'

Kurt grunted and took the hull MP40, clambering up into the howling wind. In the bright light of the burning Russian boat, I saw him approach the various smouldering bodies carefully, and prod them with his gun. On one body, he leaned down and pulled the man's felt boots off, a sought-after trophy if they were new and the right size.

He looked around some more, in the light of the blazing boat now sinking onto the river bed, the water steaming around it. He shook his head.

He came back to the panzer, and as he approached, he looked at me through the vision block, waving his new felt boots triumphantly. No prisoners, but a warm pair of feet for the night. Then his head was shattered, and parts of his skull and brains spurted sideways against the flames. Liquid from his head splattered over my vision block, tinted a violent red by the light, and other spurts came from his throat and chest as bullets pierced his torso. Kurt sprawled down under the front plate of the Tiger and disappeared from my view.

Not Kurt.

Big, ugly Kurt.

Behind him, the Ivan who had given away his comrades' location stood with his machine pistol steaming, trying to change the magazine, his crumpled cigarette still between his lips.

'Run him down, driver,' Helmann ordered.

'Kurt is in front of the panzer,' I said.

'He is dead. Run down that Ivan now.'

'But Kurt is in front of the panzer.'

Helmann swore, and the Russian swayed on his feet, looking drunk or stunned – probably both. The cupola hatch opened, and there was a one-second burst of MP40. The Russian span around, and crumpled into the reeds.

We put Kurt on the hull top, and returned slowly to the bridge bunkers, although I was not at all sure what we were going to do with his body. In the end, I put the plundered felt boots on Kurt's feet, and we buried him in a snowdrift on the river bank, smoothing the snow over his shattered face. Helmann said a few words.

'This man died to defend Europe from the threat of Russia, and to defend the Reich from Bolshevism and destruction. That is the highest duty of a German man. We are all proud of him.'

Then we took the Russian prisoner woman back into our Tiger, and took one of the Tiger crew who had lost their vehicle, to serve as a replacement radio man and hull gunner. After that, we waited for the dawn, when the Reds would come to the crossing point.

—

Around two in the morning, with the wind rising and falling over our armour plate, I fell asleep for a few minutes. I was back in our apartment in Munich, at the kitchen table, and my mother was heating milk on the stove to make *Pfannkuchen*, the pancakes with little webs of melted sugar. My father was reading the evening paper, and my sister was teasing me because a girl at school had sent me a note under the desk.

Then the memory came of the apartment block flattened by the bombing, a great pyramid of rubble, full of multi-coloured blocks from the wallpaper and the paint inside the many rooms. My family were under there, somewhere.

'*I speak German.*'

The voice was very close to me, and it seemed a strange thing for someone to be saying in Munich, even in a dream.

I said, 'What?'

'I speak German.'

It was a faint whisper.

I opened my eyes.

The controls of the Tiger loomed up in front of me, lit by the faint turret lamp. The wind was making a horrendous noise over the hull, and for a moment I thought I mistook its sound for someone's voice. Over the bulkhead, our new radio man appeared to be asleep with his face against the hull wall.

'I speak German.'

It was the Russian woman speaking to me, in German, from behind my seat position, with her mouth very close to my ear. I could feel her breath.

'Do you understand me?' she whispered.

I nodded, reaching for the MP40 beside me.

'Your commander is out of the vehicle,' she whispered, so faintly that I could barely hear her over the wind. 'And the other crew are asleep now.'

'Who are you?' I said.

'I don't want to burn.'

'I asked who you are.'

'I'm not important. I have no knowledge of anything important. But this tank will burn when the Soviets attack. I don't want to burn in here.'

Our radio/MG man grunted in his sleep, and I heard Wilf and the pilot moving in the turret. Were they asleep, perched on their narrow seats, or were they working on the gun? Could they hear anything over the howl of the wind? Was Helmann really out of the panzer?

I turned to look at the woman behind me. She was straining forward, one hand chained again to the turret ring. Yes, if the Tiger caught fire, she would be trapped in the hull, chained to its carcass. Helmann would rather let that happen than risk his valuable asset on the lawless paths of the retreat.

'How do you know German?' I whispered.

'I have an education,' she said. 'Please don't let me burn. You're a good man.'

I turned away from her, and stared at the snow through the vision block.

A good man?

Was she right about that?

The same month that my family were killed in the bombing, I shot a British prisoner in Sicily. At Kharkov, I watched while my unit burned the peasants' houses and drove them away with rifle butts, leaving the dead scattered in the fields. At Kursk, I saw our shells land on a Russian ambulance convoy, and smash it to nothing.

Once, I waited in my Tiger while Polish civilian prisoners filled craters in a road in front of us. Those that died were thrown into the holes among the earth and rocks, and then we drove forward over the new road.

How was I a good man?

'Go to sleep,' I said. 'The battle will come soon enough.'

I heard her settle back against the turret cage, her chain clinking.

Outside, the wind was dropping slightly, and the snowfall was becoming thinner. Helmann came back in, and kicked the radio operator to wake him. They began trying the radio frequencies, seeking to raise Divisional command. Helmann glanced at the Russian woman as he leaned over the radio man's shoulder, then at me.

'Did she cause any trouble?'

'No, Herr Ober.'

I kept quiet after that. I didn't tell him that the girl spoke German. After all, her time with the interrogators would come soon enough, and there was no sense in complicating our situation in the panzer. That's what I told myself.

—

We had no further sleep, and my drowsy memory of home faded like smoke. Helmann's contact with Divisional command became animated, then heated, and finally optimistic. I heard him talking about a regiment of Panthers arriving at dawn, about a Nebelwerfer rocket mortar unit that would decimate any Russian attack, about squadrons of cannon-Stukas that would hold off a rush on the crossing point.

Finally, he called me, Wilf, the other two Tiger commanders and the Flak wagon boys together in the artillery bunker. The lights in there had failed, and a single kerosene lamp hung from the concrete roof. The artillery officer was there, and also the commanders of the six Panther tanks that were dug in along the approaches.

'Midday,' Helmann said. His cat-like grey eyes glinted with ferocity. 'The Divisional command assures me that by midday tomorrow, we will have massed German armour on the western bank. There will be Panthers, Stugs and a Nebelwerfer rocket battery at the minimum; possibly 88mm PAK and more Tigers from fresh regiments. The Reds will never be able to cross against us here, with all that armour. We must hold the Reds off from the bridge until then – only until midday. We will guard the movement of the last of our forces across the river. When our armour comes, we ourselves will withdraw across the bridge and blow it. The Reds will be stuck here on this side, unable to cross against us, while our defences build up in the plain to the west. In this way will safeguard the plateau to the west, and ultimately the frontier of the Reich.'

'So we are to be heroes,' the artillery officer said in a flat voice. 'Just until midday. Very well, this appears to be our destiny. The bridge is fitted with aircraft bombs all along its superstructure, inside the columns themselves. I will set a timing mechanism to detonate them at midday. Nothing can then prevent the demolition or delay it. Even if we are all killed, the bombs will still blow at 12.00.'

Helmann expressed his approval of this plan.

'But what about your prisoner,' the artillery man said, 'your valuable asset?'

The Panther commanders looked at Helmann with interest.

'We have a valuable prisoner?' one of them said. 'Where is he?'

'The prisoner is in my Tiger and will remain there,' Helmann said, adjusting his cap. 'When we withdraw over the bridge, and the situation to the west is stabilised, I will hand the prisoner to the correct intelligence officers. The prisoner is an asset and cannot be allowed to go to the west in this confused situation at present.'

'You keep a prisoner in your vehicle during a battle, Herr Oberleutnant?' the Panther man said, genuinely mystified. 'That is unorthodox.'

'The prisoner is nobody's concern but mine. *Your* concern is holding the bridge, gentlemen,' Helmann said. His persona was very powerful; more than a product of his rank, he radiated audacity and determination, and a feline cleverness that inspired confidence. 'We hold until midday – or we fall in the attempt. We must be ready for the attack at any time, before dawn possibly. I know for a fact that the eyes of the Division, of the highest authorities, of Germany itself are on this bridge today.'

At his throat, his Iron Cross gleamed in the kerosene light.

—

In fact, the assault began at dawn itself, as the light paled slightly, showing the transformed landscape outside our Tiger. I opened the hatch and peered out at the sight.

Our three Tigers were positioned in a triangle around the approach to the bridge, facing the rising ground that we had retreated down the day before. The entire slope, stretching several kilometres north and south along the banks, and for a kilometre up to the ridge, was a perfect sheet of white, crossed in places by the tracks of the straggling vehicles and men hurrying down through the snow to the river. The snow was some two metres deep, as Kurt had predicted. In places, drifts of several metres had built up against abandoned trucks or on the boulders that dotted the area.

In front of our Tigers, spread to left and right, were the six Panthers and two Panzer IV tanks, dug into scrapes in the ground and now up to their hull tops in snow. They practised reversing out of their emplacements, to ensure they could manoeuvre if needed, and then settled in again, the air above their engines distorted with sudden heat.

Behind us, the two concrete bunkers that covered the bridge access had two 75mm PAK guns in embrasures, and multiple MG points in loopholes. There were various 20mm single Flak guns in sandbagged posts to either side. Behind the bunkers, there was a mortar platoon, and then, dug in along the river sides, shivering and hunched, were several platoons of infantry pulled together as a scratch unit. These were our remaining Panzergrenadiers, plus dismounted panzer crews, artillery men with only rifles, all thrown together in sandbagged trenches to await the onslaught. Our friendly Flak Wagon was sited among them, its four cannons raised skyward in readiness.

The bridge was still streaming with foot-soldiers and vehicles – many in bad shape, with frozen faces and barely able to walk, having struggled through the snow to escape the advancing Reds. We questioned many of them, and they told us of massed lines of heavy armour, Katyushas and ferocious infantry that took no prisoners.

I felt little emotion, watching them pass under our gun barrel. If I was mourning Kurt, I was doing it in a secret part of my heart that even I couldn't feel. I felt numb and indifferent, and I wanted to get the fighting over.

As the emerging light showed up the contours of the slope in front of us in a mauve-coloured relief, I saw a final Panzer IV appear at the top of the ridge and begin trying to make its way down to us. I focussed my binoculars on it. It evidently had engine trouble, as it was belching oil smoke and its front transmission covers were open.

'Come on, poor little friend,' my new MG man said on my right. 'Come to breakfast.'

We were all sucking on pieces of dried fruit from packets we had picked up in the retreat. I gave a packet to the Russian woman behind me, and she looked into my eyes as she raised it to her mouth with her chained hands. Looking up again at that lame-duck Panzer IV on the ridge, I squinted as a series of shapes appeared on the skyline above it.

They were tiny, box-shaped objects, vehicles of some sort, mounted on lengthy skis and driven – I realised as more of them appeared on the ridge – by an aero propeller facing to the rear. Some kind of motorised sled, crude but perfectly suited to travelling on the snow, they raced over the white surface with an ease that made a mockery of the Panzer IV's stumbling progress. Five in total, they swooped and glided across the snow, descending on the German panzer like hyenas surrounding a wounded animal.

'Hold your fire,' Helmann ordered. 'Save our shells for the Stalins. That panzer is no use to us anyway.'

It was cruel, but it was necessary. All our panzers, short on ammunition, held fire – even the PAK in the bunkers behind us, who would be key in holding back the Stalin machines when they appeared. So it was that we stood and watched as the motorised sledges surrounded the panzer on the high slope, dodging its feeble MG fire, until one sled got close enough to get in behind the panzer's rear plate. The sledge gave out a flash, and a sparking projectile flew out to strike the Panzer IV in the back hull. This was an infantry anti-tank rocket, no doubt – the type the Americans called the bazooka and we called the Panzerfaust. A hollow-headed explosive charge that could smash a hole in almost any armour. I saw the impact rip off the panzer's exhaust cover and send it whirling across the snow, and then the rocket detonated inside the engine compartment, blowing open the grilles in a shower of flames and smoke.

The panzer halted and rotated its turret rapidly, firing off long bursts of MG from the gun mantle as it ground to a halt, but the motor sledges were fast and kept away from the arc of fire. As flames spread from the engine to the lower hull, and the running gear was blazing with gasoline fire, the panzer crew jumped from the hatches and began running towards us down the slope. Even had we been allowed to fire now, it would have been impossible to aim between the running men in their dark overalls and the sleds that chased them and toyed with them as they fled. One crewman fired an MP40, but the prows of the Russian machines seemed to be armoured, as the bullets had no effect – and he was cut down under the skis, his body left crumpled in the snow. One by one, the other crew were run down by these strange, armoured sledges, their rear-facing propellers whirling and their skis slicing like sabres across the surface.

One of the Panthers could take no more, and fired off two rounds of high-explosive, but this hit one of the sledges only after it had mown down the final crew man. The sledge was blown apart, and the bodies of its operators lay burning in the white shrouded slope, alongside the bodies of the panzer men they had just killed.

The remaining sleds raced back up the slope, too fast to hit, and vanished over the crest, their skis lifting metres into the air as they leapt over the white summit.

'While they played their games, they took a good look at us, of course,' Wilf said from the turret. 'They know our disposition and strength now.'

I heard the characteristic sound of Helmann swigging from his hip flask; the noise of his swallowing was loud over his throat intercom. In a minute, the flask was thrown down to the MG man and me, and I swigged the cognac gratefully. I glanced over my shoulder, and threw the flask to the Russian woman chained to the turret bars. She drank eagerly, until the Luftwaffe pilot reached down from the turret and grabbed it back from her with a curse. We needed that drink, because, as the liquor warmed our veins, the Ivan attack began in earnest.

The sky in the east was a deep red colour, shot through with clouds of black and silver. Out of that sky, Sturmovik aircraft came down from high altitude: about a dozen black outlines against the dawn, trailing pearlescent vapour. I saw tracer from the Flak wagon shoot up to meet them, and then more from the single Flak cannons around the bunkers, all stabbing up at the angry, crimson sky.

One Sturmovik was hit in the wings, and it span over on its back – colliding with its comrade alongside. The two aircraft disintegrated, with the armoured compartments of the fuselage plummeting down, and the wings spinning away across the river. The debris was scattered over a wide area, burning brightly on the snow, but the other ten planes did not deviate by a metre. In seconds, they were on us, and releasing from their undersides a huge number of small bombs which screeched down at 45 degrees into our positions.

There were so many of these bomblets that they formed a rolling wave of fire and shrapnel, coming towards the bridge in a carpet of explosion. Many of the bombs landed wide of us, but one load was deadly accurate, and hit a Panther, covering it in smoke and soil. The bombs continued to break around us, making our Tiger hull ring out with the detonations, and slamming into the bunkers, the troop trenches and the bridge itself.

Our Flak fell silent, and no sooner did these Sturmoviks leave, banking over our heads to follow the river north, than a fresh wave came hurtling from the eastern sky. Our Flak fired again, but was ineffective, and our positions took the full force of the bomblets. The small pods were scattered among us as plentifully as dark seeds, raising flowers of flame and steel that tore between our vehicles.

Our armour plate rocked and shrieked as the debris struck, and through the vision port I could see, to left and right, the effect on the other vehicles. One of the two Panzer IVs was hit on the turret, blowing away the turret side hatches. Another bomb fell directly against the open hatch, and as the smoke cleared I saw that the inside of the turret was a chaos of flames and bodies, as ammunition exploded under the writhing figures of the crew.

A Panther was hit also, and the bomb deflected off the front plate without exploding, spinning off into the river behind us. The next moment, though, that panzer was hit by two more bombs, which broke off its cupola and smashed open the engine deck. I saw the commander's head still in the open ring where the cupola had been, pouring with blood, and the remainder of the crew struggling out of their hatches as the engine began to roar with gasoline flames. Just as the crew stood on the hull, and tried to extricate their commander, one final bomb broke over them, dismembering each man in a whirlwind of fragments.

Pieces of stone, earth and shrapnel continued to crash onto our panzer for a long time. When this finally ceased, I had to open my hatch to clear a mound of soil from in front of my port. As I pushed it clear, I quickly looked around our positions.

Our three Tigers were still in one piece; one Panther and one Panzer IV were destroyed and burning fiercely, becoming pyres for their crews. Our other armoured comrades were battered but still functioning. The bunkers had been hit, but the bombs had made cracks in the concrete without penetrating, or bounced off the roof into the infantry trench areas. One slit trench of our troops had been decimated, and their bodies, thrown out of their dugouts by the blast, lay smouldering on the snow. Our Flak Wagon, and the other Flak guns, seemed to be still intact.

Behind the bunkers, the bridge was empty now: strewn with debris but still standing. I looked forward to being on the opposite bank at midday, to see the bridge being blown up to frustrate the Red advance. We had about four hours to go. I wiped down the outside of my glass block, and slid back down into my seat. As the morning sky erupted into slabs of red and gold above the eastern ridge, tank destroyers came for us.

'My God,' I heard Wilf say in the turret. 'See these monsters.'

Looking through his gun sight, he had the best view of all of us, but with my binoculars I could observe some true beasts labouring over the crest of the ridge and slumping down with their gun barrels directed at the river. These were the self-propelled guns named the 'Soviet Union' or 'SU' destroyers: huge 15cm battleship guns mounted on T34 running gear, armoured with colossal front plates and curved gun mantles, bigger than anything we Germans had ever produced. The Russian prisoners called them the 'cat-hunters,' because they killed Tigers and Panthers. There were at least a dozen of these things on the ridge, traversing their tracks left and right in plumes of snow as they positioned their fixed guns to sight down on us.

We fired the first shots, I am pleased to say.

Wilf opened fire at once, sending his red tracer straight up the slopes, through the smoke from the burning Sturmoviks, and into the front plate of an SU gun. I saw the round deflect and go cork-screwing off over the ridge, its tracer still glowing. Wilf fired again in barely two seconds, and I had to grudgingly admire the determination of the Luftwaffe pilot acting as our loader, serving and reloading the breech skilfully, despite my hatred of his character. This time, the round hit the SU monster in its track, and threw the drive wheel twenty metres across the snow, dragging track links with it. The SU fired its gun anyway, a green tracer that flipped down from the heights, skidded across the snow for hundreds of metres – and slammed into the side of a Panther, knocking off the slim armour plates that covered the wheel tops.

Wilf laughed, and Helmann joined him, and the MG man beside me did the same. Our Tiger echoed with the stressed, frightened laughter of men facing a massive enemy, and over the laughter there was the suppressed sobbing of the Russian woman chained behind me.

After this release of tension, though, we all shut up – because the other SU beasts began firing down at us. Their shells sparked with white smoke and green tracer, and from their elevated position they took aim at us as if we were ducks sitting on a white pond. They were firing high-explosive, I realised, as I saw one round burst in the snow near us – not with the small thump of anti-tank rounds, but the explosive shock wave of a munitions round. The blast from that high calibre shell rocked our vehicle from one side to the other, and I heard shrapnel hitting our sides with the same force as 75mm shells.

We fought a stand-off duel with these beasts for several minutes. We hit one of them quickly, sending the gun mantle slumping down, and then piercing the front plate beside the tracks. The roof of its hull lifted away, and a vast amount of ammunition exploded out from inside – the big naval shells screaming around across the ridge.

We hit another SU through the front slope, and the whole vehicle began to career down the hill out of control, trailing smoke and burning oil from under its tracks. It accelerated, with the driver obviously dead or paralysed at the controls, bouncing and lifting over the mounds of snow until it rose up over a boulder and flipped onto one side, spilling burning fuel across the white surface. The crew that emerged were shot down by MG from our infantry trenches, no doubt eager for revenge after the Sturmovik assault.

We took hits in return, though. Keeping the Tiger stationary, I looked left and right through my glass, and I saw a Panther in the forward positions in front of us being struck on the turret by one of these huge shells. The explosion caused the whole turret structure to separate from the hull, and flip over onto its side. The exposed turret ring was crammed with the slumped bodies of the crew, the loader still clutching a 75mm shell in his hands. The shell exploded even as he held it, blowing him into pieces which tumbled over the panzer and fell onto the snow. The rest of the crew burned in the hull, covered in the seeping gasoline.

Craning my neck around, I could just see the edge of our bridge bunker being hit repeatedly by these shells, each one sending chunks of concrete up into the crimson-coloured sky. A Flak 20mm was hit, and the two crew were splintered along with their cannon, while their stock of cannon magazines detonated, sending white tracer in a spray across the river.

Another SU was hit by our elevated fire, the great machine retreating a few metres in clouds of smoke and then boiling up in twists of red fire. Now the PAK in the bunkers behind us came to life, and found the range properly, shooting up another of the SUs with shots through the hull nose and the tracks. The top of the ridge was so steep, and the SUs were inclined downwards at such an angle, that our shots were falling on their less exposed upper surfaces, with some creditable results.

One more SU was immobilised, with a shot into its front hull that sent bits of its transmission crashing out in a spray of oil. Its comrades, though, knew our weaknesses, and concentrated their fire on the Panthers. As this frantic exchange of fire ended, a Panther was hit on the front plate in a colossal explosion of metal fragments.

The Panther immediately reversed, its driver clearly seeking to take it away from the line of fire. As it careered backwards past our position, I saw why: the whole frontal glacis plate of the panzer

WOLFGANG FAUST

was ripped off and hanging loose, leaving the body of the MG man hanging out of the front, and the face of the driver exposed to the Russian fire. The Panther reversed and skidded, and came to rest with its rear plate up against the wall of one of the bunkers. There, as the driver wriggled and flailed in his seat, it was shot to pieces by more SU fire, splitting the hull and smacking the turret around against the concrete.

I grimaced, clenched my fists, and looked up again at the slope. I was beyond thinking or feeling – I wanted only to know what the next weapon was that would be sent against us. All I saw, as the SU machines paused their fire for a while, was a ragged, scrambling group of infantry – German infantry – emerge from snowdrifts on the lower slope and begin to run down the hill towards us.

These were men who had obviously buried themselves as the battle erupted, now encrusted with snow and possessed with a desire to flee the Russians that evidently overcame their exhaustion and the icicles which clung to their faces and uniforms. Flinging aside their weapons – even the precious heavy machine guns across their shoulders – these desperate scarecrows stumbled through the snow, disappearing as they fell headlong, and dragging themselves out of the drifts in their race for safety.

Behind them, a final Hanomag half-track emerged from under a bank of snow, and sought to plough its way down the slope, with its armoured nose chewing at the mounds. It travelled fifty metres before one of SU rounds caught it, and flung it into the air. As it rose, I saw that it had the red cross of the medical orderlies on the side – it was a heavy-duty ambulance. The hull broke open, and scattered its load of wounded men across the slope – and then crashed on top of them in a cloud of smoke, rolling over and over, each turn crushing another helpless man.

The fleeing infantry broke into a crazy scramble, with men falling behind and stretching out their arms for help while their comrades scrabbled through the snow, in places up to their waists, and then in a drift up to their necks. There was nothing they could do

100

to make progress in that depth, and as they stopped, with only their heads visible, some SU shells burst among them.

I am sure that I was not the only panzer man who closed his eyes, bunched his hands and refused to look at the carnage that took place. When the shelling stopped, I wiped the condensation from my glass block and looked again.

The soldiers buried up to their necks in the snow had all been decapitated.

The naked, severed stumps of their necks projected red above the white surface, still steaming in their final energy.

There followed a moment of low cursing from Helmann, followed by barked commands. The SU monsters on the ridge remained stationary, but snow flew up in spirals as the Stalin tanks came over the crest to join the battle.

The massive, block-shaped glacis plates of the Stalins, the shapes that I had seen before, stood out in horrible clarity now, stark against the snow beneath them and the crimson dawn sky above. Our gunners, always alert, took aim at them as their underbellies rose over the crest, and pierced one under the hull between the tracks. I saw the round punch through the lower plate and emerge from the upper hull, carrying with it the upper hatch cover and the severed limbs of crew men up into the red sky.

That was only one strike, however - and the other massive steel beasts crashed down onto the slopes and took only a moment to get their bearings before heading down for the bridge.

They were in a powerful position above us, while we were static targets. On the other hand, their long gun barrels were lifting and falling as their tracks ploughed across the snow and the pointed hull fronts rose and fell. Their shots against us went wide, their tracer shooting out across the river or slamming into the bunkers with hollow detonations.

Our shells were carefully chosen, timed to strike against the great turrets of the Stalins as they rose and fell, and we blew the turret off the leading attacker as it stormed towards us in a spiral of exhaust fumes. The great turret structure reared up, crackling with fire, and then fell down loose, the gun barrel spinning around as the hull drove on regardless. Another 88mm round shot its track off, and then the Panthers hit it with their 75mm rounds, smashing holes in the prow that had the machine leaving a trail of wheels, track links and burning oil behind it as it finally came to a halt.

The numbers were too great, however, and our ammunition was too limited. Time and again, I heard Helmann and Wilf consulting in the turret, considering whether this shot or that shot was a good use of the few rounds that we had left. More often than not, Helmann held Wilf back from firing, and at other times we shot and had some success against the attackers of the Reich.

The Panthers, too, had their successes, using their static firing platforms to strike at the rolling, tipping Stalin tanks which could not stabilise their barrels against us properly. I saw one Panther rip the track and wheels off a Stalin with three rapid shells, punching in along the lower hull when the vehicle rose up out of the snow. The Stalin went out of control, and turned over onto its roof, while another Panther fired into its other flank, blowing its engine out of the back plate and releasing a wave of fuel that ignited in a flash, brighter than the dawn above the ridge.

The Stalins, however, seemed to have no fear or sense of danger. One came thumping its way up to us across the snow, firing as it reached shallower drifts and its wallowing lessened. One of its rounds smashed into our front plate, and the impact damaged my leg, as the suspension arm beside me rocked back and belted me hard. The pain shot up my spine and made me grunt, and I had my eyes closed in pain as Wilf fired back at this intruder with the 88mm.

When I opened my eyes, the Stalin was on fire in front of us, with its turret dislocated and orange flames licking around it. But another round hit us, and then another, and I heard Helmann shouting through the intercom for me to move our panzer up onto the plain, to get in among the Stalins. I shook myself, but the action sent pain through my neck and cerebellum. I felt heat on my chin, and slowly tasted blood. I felt something in my throat, and I almost choked on a broken tooth.

'Move the panzer, you driver,' Helmann was yelling. 'We must be mobile, damn you, Faust.'

I looked up, and saw bright, red sky. A Russian armour-piercing round had knocked off my hatch cover, smashing my face with shrapnel but leaving me otherwise untouched. I laughed like a madman, looking up at the sky. I felt Helmann's boot in my back two or three times, and then I saw our MG man reaching for me over the bulkhead, past the useless instrument panel. He was holding some kind of capsule, with a needle attached, and he plunged it into my arm through my tunic.

'Kurt?' I mumbled. 'Kurt, you're back. What did they do to you?'

The radio man slapped my face repeatedly. 'I'm not Kurt. That injection will do you good, Faust,' he yelled. 'Now drive us, for God's sake. We cannot sit here with these Reds around us.'

The injection did me good – a lot of good. Afterwards, I guessed it was a small dose of morphine mixed with a high dose of amphetamine, which was a familiar cocktail in the army for lightly wounded men. It kept them fighting and pain-free – and it certainly did that for me. All the pain in my head and neck subsided, and I spat out another bloody tooth without even feeling it. I found that I seemed to be using the driving controls with astonishing expertise, even if my lurching movements made Helmann shout in protest as we raced up violently onto the plain below the ridge, to meet the JS tanks that were charging down to the river.

Around us, the Panthers and even the surviving Panzer IV were moving too, because the Stalins were so close that to be static was to invite destruction. The Panthers rolled out of their emplacements, then traversed skilfully to meet the threat, their exhausts flaring and their muzzle brakes streaming with smoke as they began firing.

The Panzer IV came up onto the plain and stayed there, traversing and firing rapidly, a panzer design from the 1930's suddenly exposed to the weapons of the future. It loosed off a series of rounds, which I saw with my newly energised vision. Then I saw the little panzer break apart as Stalin shells tore up its hull, breaking off its turret cladding and rocking the brave machine over on its side. The turret blew off, as the Stalin shells that destroyed it pierced its sides and exited out of the empty turret ring, setting off the fuel in its rear tanks. Long plumes of burning gasoline span after the exiting rounds, turning the snow into a vaporous mass.

The Panthers fought back calmly, rationally, seeking their prey with their long-barrelled 75mm guns, and picking off weak points in the Stalin tanks' armour. I weaved the Tiger across the plain, watching a JS blow apart in front of me, a German round splitting the lip between its turret and hull, and exiting out of the engine deck in a spray of burning fuel.

Wilf in our turret hit one JS, and then another, but our rounds deflected from their oblong turrets without piercing them. We hit a third Stalin, blowing off the gun mantle and putting another round into its hull side as it span around. Plumes of fire issue from its broken turret as our round ricocheted within there before exploding.

At the same time, though, we took our losses.

The Tiger on our right was hit through the turret side, and the shell exited up through the commander's cupola, dragging with it the black-uniformed torso of the commander himself. The panzer was hit in the wheels next, and several of the great steel discs flew away behind it as the vehicle lurched over onto its side, coming to rest at an angle which exposed its belly plate to the Stalins. The Red tanks shot into this target repeatedly, until the rounds punching through from the underside shot away the entire turret, and explosions erupted from the empty ring space.

With our two remaining Tigers and a handful of Panthers, we fought the Stalin attack to a standstill. I drove the Tiger with the clumsy confidence of a man stimulated by drugs, taking it from one part of the battlefield to another, moving and halting for Wilf to fire off a number of shots at the Russian machines. Even when the

Stalins were immobilised, they continued to fire at us, using their tanks as metal bunkers amid the snow.

One such tank shot at us with a maniacal speed, its tracer rounds flashing past us as we manoeuvred around it to put a shell in from its side. Our 88mm round went exactly centre, just above the snow-covered tracks. The turret hatch lifted up and detonating ammunition spiralled out into the red-tinged sky, adding to the smoke pouring across the stained, rutted snow. Even then, the driver's hatch opened and a crew man emerged, still in his protective headgear, holding a machine pistol. He fired on us with the little gun, the bullets pattering on our front armour, until our hull MG man brought him down with a single shot. Every round had to count now, had to find its mark; while every manoeuvre and evasion used up our dwindling fuel.

I lost track of time in that fight, with my head spinning from the amphetamines and my body unaware of pain. I noticed, with a strange detachment, that the sky was whitening, and the sun was now looming over the ridge above us. It was a fierce, crimson sun, casting jagged shadows from the peaks, and lighting the scattered wrecks of panzers that burned around us.

In its light, the Stalins withdrew up the slope, reversing rapidly, firing as they left. Our 75mm PAK in the bunkers caught one of them with repeated hits as it lurched backwards in the snow, smashing off the very tip of its pointed hull. The Red tank kept on reversing, with two crewmen visible inside the hull through the split-open front. Wilf was unable to resist the temptation: he fired directly into the exposed compartment. Cool as always, he had selected high-explosive, and the detonation of the shell deep inside the confined steel box blew out the driver and machine-gunner from the fractured hull, sending them cartwheeling across the snow, trailing smoke. The Stalin's ruptured compartment became an inferno of orange flames, in which other men were visible, struggling and writhing, until the vehicle was enveloped in its own smoke.

The firing stopped. The sky darkened to a blue steel colour, in which the ascendant sun was a red disc, issuing out bands of fiery light. I guessed that the next wave of the Red assault would be barely a few minutes away.

—

This lull was full of rapid activity in our ranks. Our two Tigers checked ammunition and fuel: we had thirty rounds between us, and enough fuel for ten minutes driving, and then to reverse across the bridge. Our four surviving Panthers had similar reserves, we learned over the radio, and the PAK officers ran down from the bunkers for a brief consultation beside our hull.

They still had substantial reserves of armour-piercing, and the mortar battery behind the bunker line had not yet fired a shot. The Flak guns had reasonable reserves, but the infantry in their slit trenches were low on everything – ammunition, spirit and strength.

Helmann regrouped our vehicles into a ragged half-circle around the crossing point, with the bunkers literally at our backs, the steel bridge glinting in the red sunlight.

In all the activity, and the grinding of gears, the rattle of the machines as we positioned the panzers, I heard the Russian woman behind me murmur from beside my ear.

'All this destruction, what is the purpose?'

Our radio man glanced at her with a frown, evidently not hearing her words but concerned at her communication with me.

'We are defending Europe,' I said to her.

'Like this?' She laughed bitterly – then, seeing the radio man look at her again, she sank back to her crouching position under the turret.

My reply to her had been instinctive, a slogan but a genuinely felt one, the reason that we had come to this country and unleashed the slaughter we brought. The drugs in my system were still active, and I felt confident, strangely invulnerable. The radio man grinned at me – and offered me another amphetamine boost, this time in the form of a *Pervitin* tablet in a foil wrapper. These nitrate pills were widespread in our forces, and I crunched this one between my teeth and swallowed it.

'Panzer sweets!' our MG man laughed, taking two for himself.

My vision became narrower, but more acute, and I saw the red sunlight among the fires on the snow in a brilliant hue that I had not noticed before. The hairs on my scalp bristled. My sense of smell also became more acute, and the reek of explosive and fuel in the hull was painful. I raised my face to the open hatch to gulp some fresh air. I could see up to the ridge top, and the SU self-propelled guns up there were manoeuvring to the left and right, as if making way for a new presence.

With my binoculars, I studied the ridge, and in a moment called a warning up to Helmann that the Reds were attacking again.

'Ja,' he murmured, 'I see them too. Katyushas again, but many of them. Fire on them when they stop moving, gunner,' he said to Wilf. 'Use high explosive, we have more of that.'

'Sir,' Wilf said.

'Just one more hour!' Helmann exhorted his crews over the radio. 'We must hold for one more hour, then our reinforcements will be on the river, and we will withdraw.'

Another hour of this fury? An hour of Katyushas?

The Katyushas, I saw through my field glasses, were mounted on tracked carriers which had laboured over the ridge, belching exhaust. The vehicles carried sets of launcher racks loaded with finned rockets, aiming them crudely by pointing the vehicles' noses down the slope at us, and then angling the racks up and down by hand. As they did this, Wilf immediately fired on them, and his tracer tore into a pair of these machines as the crews were making their adjustments. Their rockets detonated on the racks, and a colossal fireball blew up over the vehicles, obliterating them and their teams. The fire expanded, coiling into many spirals that flexed, rose and fell as it spread, causing the surrounding trucks to scatter frantically out of the way.

The Russians set off smoke flares to conceal their activity, and in moments, the upper part of the ridge was shrouded in a thick, brown smoke. Our PAKS in the bunkers shot into the smoke, but apparently without hitting anything, and we held our fire, the smokescreen was so dense. Even through the smoke, though, the flickering glow of that strange fire continued to burn and expand.

'*Scheisse*,' Helmann muttered. 'That is gasoline jelly.'

'What is that?' I heard the Luftwaffe pilot say, his voice trembling.

'Gasoline and diesel in a viscous form, mixed with tyre rubber,' Helmann said, without emotion. 'It will stick to anything, and it burns for hours.'

The pilot began praying to himself, until Helmann told him to shut up.

'They will have observers lower down on the slopes,' Helmann said to us all. 'They will fire through the smoke and –'

As he said the words, the first of the Katyusha projectiles came screaming down the hillside towards us. Even to my drugged and over-stimulated senses, the rockets were a spectacular and terrifying sight. They shot out of the brown smoke in salvos of a dozen, the whole salvo taking barely a few seconds. The smoke formed into horizontal tornados in their slipstream, filled with the sparks that flew from the base of the long, dart-shaped weapons themselves. The projectiles flew wide at first, shooting way off along the river bank north of the bridge, and exploding there in a wall of coiling fire that grew to the height of a church tower, covering hundreds of metres of land. The observers were quick to correct this, however, and the next round of salvos came down on the area around the bridge.

We were all brave men in that panzer, but I was not the only one, I am sure, who pleaded with fate to spare him the impact of these dreadful flames. I was glad that our female prisoner could not see the attack; but to hear the screech of the rockets around us, and to inhale the stench of their rubberised fuel were bad enough.

Some rockets flew over our heads, and I heard Helmann say that they hit the opposite bank behind us. Others caught a Panther on the outer edge of our group, and the whole vehicle was consumed in a ball of those boiling flames. Death for that crew must have been by roasting, as the fires intensified and burned, and the blazing, sticking liquid dripped down into the hull through any vent or crack.

One storm of rockets exploded directly in front of us, and I saw the finned tubes disintegrate and release their incendiary load, which spread out in a nightmarish web of burning tendrils that seemed to probe the landscape for a victim to consume. I reversed at an angle away from the flames, and the change in position gave me a fuller viewpoint of the effect of the rockets on our defences.

The burning Panther was a dim outline in its pillar of flames. The other Panthers were standing firm, as was our fellow Tiger – but the bunkers themselves were on fire from the Katyusha strikes. One had its roof ablaze, and burning liquid was gushing down into the embrasures. I could see the PAK crews in there, working with extinguishers to preserve their guns. The other bunker was on fire all down one wall, and the flames had splashed onto a Flak position also. The crew were rolling in the snow, covered in fire, and the 20mm tracer rounds were shooting wildly as they detonated. Behind the bunkers, the river itself was on fire, as the incendiary material floated on the water, sending up clouds of steam while the flames expanded from one bank to the other. The bridge itself was still standing, some of its uprights drenched in flames like some kind of demonic, burning symbol rising over us.

I straightened the panzer's alignment, and looked up again at the ridge.

One more salvo of Katyushas came down, setting the ground around us ablaze, but sparing our panzers. I began to have hope that this final hour might be survivable, that Helmann's plan might be workable. After all, if we could survive this, could we not survive anything they might throw against us? Wasn't our Tiger still in one piece, and still running?

The Katyusha launchers fell silent, and beyond the gasoline flames, the brown smokescreen was thinning in the morning breeze.

As the smoke dissipated, shapes appeared within it, and I recognised the low, squat outlines of the Stalin tanks, lumbering down the slope again towards us. These were new, fresh vehicles, too, painted in grey-white winter camouflage, the red star still proudly displayed, and showing no signs of recent action. I counted twenty, then thirty of these monsters – and then I gave up counting, because the slopes were full of the machines, each with its pale paint and red star, each with its long barrel dipping and rising as they ploughed through the snow towards us.

Thirty – or forty? Or more? Against two Tigers, a handful of Panthers and some PAK in bunkers? Even if we held this wave off from the bridge, surely the Reds had another fresh company up there on the ridge, and another after that, while we had only ourselves, and our almost depleted ammunition.

'Forty-five minutes,' Helmann said. 'I believe the first of our armour reinforcements are already on the western bank.' I heard him swivelling around to check 360 degrees with his periscopes. 'Yes, we have new panzers on the western side,' he said triumphantly. 'And more than that – yes, I told you! We have Stukas with cannons.'

Stukas? With cannons?

'Yes, I see them,' the Luftwaffe pilot yelled. 'They are coming in low. Shoot well, lads. Shoot them up for us, I beg you.'

Now I saw the shadows of the Stukas racing across the snow from behind us: black, crooked shapes outlined by the overhead sun. Then the aircraft themselves appeared over our gun barrel. Six magnificent Stukas, each with a pair of long cannon slung under its wings – the same weapon that our pilot friend had been flying when he crashed beside us. I saw the planes advance, their gull wings clearly shown from behind, and the aircraft seemed to float in the air as they swooped around to attack the Red armour from the sides. In moments, the Stukas were right over the Ivan mass, and they began firing their cannon.

I was astonished at the effect.

The Stuka guns were able to fire down on the great Stalins, onto the hull and turret roofs, and above all into the engine decks to hit the thinly shielded vents over the power plant. The aircraft swooped in their distinctive, floating way, with the tracer cannon rounds firing in bursts which were short but intense. When the tracer hit the turret walls, I saw the rounds deflect off in corkscrew patterns, but where they punched through the upper surfaces or the grilles, they penetrated with the tell-tale puff of metal fragments as the shell entered the vehicle.

One Stalin erupted in flames and span around sideways in the snow, and a Panther finished the task with a 75mm round into its flank which caused the Red's gun barrel to slump into the snow as it burned. Another Stalin had its track shot away by the Stukas, and as the track links whirled around through the air, the tank collided at speed with one of its comrades, both becoming jammed together in deep snow. As the two crews began climbing out, the first men to emerge were hit by another Stuka's burst of cannon, which left the men slumped in the hatches, obstructing the exit of those still inside. Those two tanks had their engine covers blown off completely, and pieces of the engines were shot out, wreathed in burning oil.

I saw one more JS hit repeatedly, with lines of tracer flying through the forward hull roof. The hull and turret hatches opened, and thick smoke trailed out as the vehicle continued to charge forward, obviously unable to stop. It careered into a mound of snow, lifted onto its side and rolled onto its turret, which sank into the snow. Static, with its belly plate facing up and its tracks still running around uselessly, it was an easy target, and the following Stuka hammered a line of shells into its underside, causing a burst of flames to erupt around it.

'You see?' our pilot shouted from the turret. 'You see what the Stuka can do? See the Reds break up.'

Indeed, the massed charge down the gradient by the Stalins was becoming confused, with some vehicles veering off to the side in evasive action, and others colliding as they sought to avoid the hail of shells from the sky.

'Don't fire until they're closer,' Helmann ordered. 'Every shell of ours must count now. Thirty minutes more.'

My heart was pounding with a sense of impending victory, as much as with the amphetamines surging through my system. After all our struggles, Hellmann was going to be proved correct. The Reds would be held off, the bridge would be denied them, and our forces massing on the western bank would prevent them crossing here indefinitely. It was all, ultimately, worthwhile – all the shooting, the flames, the shattered bodies and spilled blood.

'Go on, my friends,' the pilot shouted, and I heard him open the loader's hatch, perhaps to get a better view of this rare triumph of the Luftwaffe. 'Go on!' he yelled from up there.

Then I realised that the success of the Stukas was purely temporary – and the bridge was in danger after all.

Our Flak began to fire, in long, weaving lines of tracer behind the passing Stukas, and by craning my neck I could just see, coming behind the German aircraft from the north, a formation of planes in the distinctive brown of the Red Air Force. These were not Sturmoviks, but true fighter planes; their speed was staggering as they raced in behind the bigger Stukas and began to fire, with the flashes of guns coming from their wings and propeller cones. They were so fast that they were through the Stukas within seconds – and now it was the German air attack which was broken up with fire.

Of the four Stukas still overhead, at an altitude of barely two hundred metres, one was set on fire immediately, with long streams of burning fuel pouring back from its wings. It rolled upside down and tumbled to earth, crashing onto one of the Stalins that had tried to swerve away from the air attack. The Stalin kept travelling, with pieces of burning aircraft trailing from it, drenched in the blazing kerosene fuel from the Stuka, until the tank ground to a halt and rocked as it also burned.

Another Stuka was pursued up and over the ridge of the heights – the last sight we had of it was a trail of black smoke and sparks as the Russian fighter shot pieces off its tailplane. A third Stuka was hit in the engine, and fragments of its propeller and cowling span down onto the battlefield. Unlike the armoured Sturmoviks, our Stukas had no metal plate to protect the crew and engine, and any rounds tore pieces from its fragile skin. That Stuka rolled around and banked out of my sight, dipping towards the river.

The fourth Stuka that I could see was torn to bits in mid-air by two fighters on its tail, their machine gun rounds chewing along its gull wings and then smashing off the glass cockpit canopy, blasting the cockpit interior. The Stuka reared up, and twisted upside down – throwing out the two crew men, who fell, writhing, to earth – striking the ground while their aircraft was still in the sky. The empty plane went rolling over to the south, with flames gushing from its nose.

Our Luftwaffe pilot shouted in despair, as his comrades' victory was turned to humiliation before his eyes. Even then, one of those Russian fighters had not finished with us, because it banked around, pursued by stabs of our Flak, and charged at us along the line of the river. Its gun rounds strafed along the infantry trenches, hit two of our Panthers harmlessly, and then hammered on the top of our hull, the echo fading quickly.

Our Flak caught that fighter almost by accident, as the plane banked into a stream of tracer, and the Red aircraft spurted a cloud of flame as its fuel exploded. The fuselage and engine soared down and went skidding along the snow like a sledge, with its pilot still inside the blazing cockpit. The wreck finally dug into the snow nose-first; its tail, with the defiant red star emblem, rose up vertically and stood burning between the two battle groups of opposing tanks.

I heard Helmann and Wilf talking urgently on the headphones, and at the same time, the Russian woman behind me began laughing in her bitter, almost hysterical way.

'Leave the body,' Helmann was saying. 'I shall load the gun now myself. We have only a few rounds left, anyway.'

'The Luftwaffe man is hit?' I asked over the intercom.

'The *verdamm* fool put his head out of the hatch,' Wilf's voice replied. 'They shot his handsome head right off his shoulders.'

I heard a crash behind me, and the Russian woman started screaming. I looked around, to see the body of the pilot – the headless body, I realised – which had just fallen from the turret hatch onto the hull floor. It lay there, spurting blood, while the prisoner scrabbled to get away from it in the confined space.

'Twenty minutes until midday,' Helmann shouted. 'The eyes of Germany are on us now.'

Our radio man glanced around at the beheaded corpse and the screaming woman.

'If the eyes of Germany could see this *scheisse*,' he muttered. 'Watch now, Faust. They are coming for us again. You see?'

Yes, the Stalins were coming for us.

With the Stukas gone, the squat machines found their momentum again, and formed up against us in a jagged, inverted circle formation. Their intention was clearly to surround us, to bring their edges in along the river bank and form a noose around us, with Reds on all sides and the river at our backs. They must be aware of our defensive reinforcements assembling on the western side – indeed, from their higher ground they could of course see our forces collecting over there – and they surely had a desperate urgency to pour across the bridge and spread out before our counter-attacking forces could resist their surge.

The Stalins came on, and Helmann in the turret was telling Wilf to *wait, wait* until they were close. Our other panzers were exercising the same discipline, and even when the Stalins began firing, we held our shots until the enemy shells were already exploding against us. I felt one Stalin round hit the outer bulkhead in front of me, and scabs of metal plate flew off and smashed against my chest. The round did not penetrate, though, although the armour where it struck was dented inwards from the impact.

In response, Wilf opened fire, and the final fight for the crossing point began with the boom of our 88mm and the straight line of our red tracer, directly into the glacis plate of a Stalin coming towards us. The Stalin lost power, and as it slowed it turned its hull flank to us. Wilf punched through it with another round, and the Stalin halted in a cloud of snow, its entire back end lifting up into the air as its running gear locked. One of the bunker PAKS shot right through the engine deck, the shell exiting underneath the tank even before its rear came back down onto the snow. A pillar of flame erupted from its back hull, and Wilf laughed softly.

Now I was a driver with nowhere to drive. The bunkers were behind us, the PAKS firing over us into the Red mass, and to left and right were our handful of comrade panzers, each of them firing now and using the last of its ammunition in these final minutes.

The Stalins began to move around us, two of them lumbering up to the very bank of the river beyond our last Panther, and firing into the Panther from the flank. I saw one round deflect off the Panther's turret – and then another round smash open the cupola, and a third break pieces off the rear hull near the engine. The Panther kept firing, as smoke and then flames issued from its rear deck; firing on and on at the attackers, even as more Stalin shells were raking into it from the flank. One final Ivan round lifted off the whole turret, which split apart and sent pieces whirling into the air. I saw the crew inside, as damaged as their proud machine, lying in the empty turret ring as the flames spread around them.

Wilf above me was firing, and Helmann was loading the breech with grunts and curses, but loading it well because we hit another Stalin in the drive wheel. The steel wheel went racing into the air and hit another Stalin, bouncing off it and rolling away across the snow.

The damaged tank shed more wheels and track, digging a long groove in the snow as it came to a halt. One of the Panthers astutely raced to its flank and shot it from the side, then rotated its turret and shot at another Stalin approaching behind it. That Stalin, I saw through my grimy glass block, was carrying a squad of infantry on its rear deck – men clinging on to hand grips on the turret. The Stalin halted, and the infantry leaped off into the snow. Wearing white winter suits, they struggled through the powder towards us, while behind them their Stalin and our Panther shot at each other from less than three hundred metres range.

The Panther was the victor there, putting a 75mm round precisely under the Stalin's gun mantle, which seemed to jam the Russian tank's turret and armament. I watched as the Panther prowled to one side, traversed its gun, and finished its opponent at point-blank range with a round into the hull.

Numbers, though, were always our enemy – numbers and lack of ammunition, and the river behind us which prevented us reversing, breaking out to the sides and flanking our enemy in a counter-attack. Instead, our Tiger remained largely static, taking hit after hit on our hull and turret while Wilf calmly aimed and fired what shells he had left.

More of the Stalins were carrying infantry now, halting to let them jump down and go to ground or to advance on us through the snow. The MG beside me spat out its rounds at them, until its smoke filled the gunner's compartment and mine. The Red troops hung back, sheltering behind the red-splattered bodies of their friends, waiting for us to be finished before they charged.

The hits on us rose to a crescendo, rounds smashing into us again and again, their resounding crash and echo accompanied by Helmann's curses and the shrieks of the Russian woman, still chained behind me with the decapitated corpse of the pilot. One Ivan round hit our front plate in the centre, and the transmission began grinding badly, with boiling lubricant spurting into my legs. My drugged body registered the pain distantly, and even when another shell hit the top of my hull and went howling off across the snow, I blinked, recognised the fact but did not flinch. I was aware that we were being steadily shot to pieces; locked into my tiny, steel compartment I waited either for the end or for orders from Helmann.

Even when a shell finally pierced our armour, and came in through the radio man's compartment wall, I only realised slowly what had happened. Fragments of white-hot metal flew across from his side, and ricocheted off the hull wall, followed by a lump of red metal which smashed off the bulkhead behind me and exited upward out of my hatch – straight up through the empty circle.

I shook myself, unable to take in the situation.

I heard the radio man groan, and then I saw him convulse, as I slowly turned my head to look at him. The Russian armour-piercing round had entered through a hole in the steel beside him, which was still smoking, and it had punched through his chest before rebounding and hitting my side of the hull. His torso was ripped open, and the steam from inside him was mingling with the smoke drifting around in the hull.

Then another round hit us, and this one split open the hull roof from the front wall, showing a scrap of the winter sky in the gap. Our Tiger was being knocked apart, blow by blow.

I felt the familiar kick in my back from Helmann's boot, and heard his voice close behind me.

'Reverse, Faust, for God's sake. We're going back over the bridge now.'

'Is it the time?' I said, stupidly.

'Reverse or I'll shoot you and drive it myself,' he said calmly. Behind him, the Russian woman was staring at me, splattered with the fresh blood of the dead Luftwaffe man.

I reversed, following shouted directions from the turret, aiming for the bridge access between the bunkers. Through the vision block in front of me, I saw one of our Panthers charging from left to right, seeking to ram a Stalin that was advancing on the bridge. The Panther was hit as it moved, the gun mantle lifting off in a starburst of sparks, and another round shooting off the entire back plate behind the engine. The engine tumbled out in a flood of burning fuel, but the panzer had enough momentum to ram the JS, knocking it sideways and partly on its side. Another Stalin rolled up alongside the two conjoined vehicles, and shot the Panther one last time through the top of the hull.

As we reversed away, I saw the Panther being shredded apart by Russian shells, fired from ten metres distance, until it was consumed in the blaze of its own fuel.

More shells hit our Tiger, and one blew away our right track, so that we could only limp back, the offside running gear jammed and dragging in the snow. In this state, I felt the back of the panzer lift onto the access ramp to the bridge. There, the transmission screamed and went suddenly quiet.

I tried the starter repeatedly – but the Maybach did not respond. The giant beast was truly dead. In the quiet, I heard the crackle of flames from the engine compartment. I jerked into life, as the smell of gasoline filled the vehicle. We had only a little fuel remaining, but what there was seemed to be seeping into the hull space – enough to incinerate us all in our steel box.

'Exit the panzer,' Helmann shouted, but I was already clambering up through my open hatch into the freezing air of the battlefield. Despite my alarm, and the shells flying past me, I stopped dead for a moment. I had witnessed disjointed parts of this battle through my driver's port – but now the full situation became clear.

The red sun was directly overhead in its metallic sky. On the plain, and on the slopes leading up to the ridge, scores of vehicles lay smashed and burning – Stalins, our panzers, and the wreckage of the other vehicles abandoned in the retreat. Wreckage of downed aircraft lay among them, both the Stukas and the tail of that crashed Russian fighter, still burning vertically, its red star now scorched away. The surviving Stalins were probing to the bunkers, and only our comrade Tiger and two Panthers remained to deny them. Coming down from the ridge, the huge SU guns were crawling towards the carnage also, determined to feast on our destruction.

Between the tanks, groups of Red infantry were advancing, exchanging murderous fire with our troops in the slit trenches. Our Flak Wagon was firing horizontally, cutting down the Reds as they tried to rush the bridge. It took one shot from an SU gun to blow the brave wagon to pieces, sending the four Flak barrels whirling through the air like straws.

Exposed as I was on the Tiger's hull, I shook myself, and ran around the Tiger's turret to shelter behind its bulk, although the engine grilles that I stood on were flickering with flames. With shock, I found that the Luftwaffe pilot's decapitated head was lying there on the rear hull, with its blue eyes staring up at the sky.

I heard the Russian woman scream from inside the hull – but then Wilf emerged, and Helmann, both scrambling out of their turrets.

'The prisoner,' I shouted. 'She is chained in there.'

'Leave her,' Wilf said. 'The panzer is finished. It's burning.'

Helmann, holding his MP40, slapped me on the back.

'You want to rescue a lady in distress?' he goaded me. 'Please go ahead.' He gave me a small key.

I looked at him, saw the way his feline grey eyes were gleaming in the light of the flames, and I dived down back through the gunner's hatch. Russian bullets were smacking on the armour around me and whining off into the snow. Inside the turret, I could just see the woman through the smoke, struggling with her chains. Beside her, the pilot's mutilated body was starting to flicker with flames as the leaking gasoline soaked his clothing.

The woman was chained to the turret bars with a handcuff clasp. I used Hellmann's key to undo this, and I pulled the chain free. Flames began to spurt from the slots of the engine bay, hissing and roaring as the engine burned fully. Russian shells crashed into the front of the Tiger and broke off more pieces – the MG ball mount, the side wall of the dead radio man's position – with deafening retorts. I grabbed the woman by the waist and hoisted her up into the turret, away from the worst of the flames, and opened the circular hatch in the turret rear.

I pushed her out of this head-first, and she wriggled and bucked to get through, into the smoke and flames coming from the engine deck. I saw Helmann grab her and pull her clear, and I followed her out. I fell onto the burning engine vents and rolled off, onto the snow at the rear. The woman, Wilf and Helmann were down there now, sheltering behind the Tiger's rear plate as the front of the panzer was demolished by enemy shots. With no ammunition left to explode, and only minimal fuel to burn off, the Tiger simply stood as a steel blockhouse, shuddering as each new round hit it.

I saw one of the Panthers hit as well, its turret blown completely away in a cascade of fragments, and the crew inside left as charred figures in the hull. The crew of the other Panther, clearly out of ammunition, jumped from their vehicle and tried to run back to the bunkers. A squad of Red infantry caught them, and bayoneted them as they ran. One of the Russians ran right past them, firing a heavy calibre gun, and he sprinted to the bridge access itself. Bullets from our infantry were pitching around him in the snow. He was hit, and slumped down next to us behind our Tiger, blood soaking through his white overalls from his thigh.

He looked at us, found he could not reach his gun, and reluctantly raised his hands in surrender. Helmann shot him in the chest with one bullet; then he turned to me, Wilf and the woman.

'I see our other Tiger is coming,' he yelled. 'We jump onto it and we cross the bridge.'

The battle around the bunkers was becoming a ragged, vicious infantry engagement now. Our mortar team behind the bunkers were firing blindly onto the plain, their rounds hitting groups of Russians as they surged forwards. Each time, the Reds climbed over the shattered bodies of their comrades while the smoke of the explosion was still in the air, and charged on. Some of our troops rose from their trenches and fought hand-to-hand with the Ivans, clubbing and slashing at each other with rifle stocks and bayonets. Other German soldiers broke and ran back to the bridge, everyone aware that its destruction was a matter of minutes now – and aware that any man left behind on the Russian side was worse than dead. Those that retreated, however, fared more badly than the ones who stayed and fought, because the Red troops brought many of them down with machine gun fire as they rushed past us.

I saw a pair of the SU guns lumber close to the bunkers, bulldozing aside a burning Panther, and begin firing at point-blank range with their colossal battleship guns into the concrete walls. Pieces of blockwork flew off and were thrown across the river, hitting those few Germans who were running headlong over the bridge.

Our second Tiger rattled close to us. Its engine was juddering and oil smoke was pouring from its vents – but it was still moving, and reversing up onto the bridge ramp. I think its commander saw us from the cupola ports, because it slowed slightly. Helmann and Wilf grabbed the crumpled track covers and swung themselves up onto the rear deck, behind the protective bulk of the turret. I grabbed the woman and threw her up there, helped by the two men, and then I clambered up to join them.

This Tiger was pitted and scarred with multiple shell strikes, its hatches partly blown off and several wheels missing on one side, making it sway wildly. On the side of the turret, an armour piercing round was embedded in the steel plate, not having penetrated through, still smoking hot. Shrapnel and bullets screeched in the air.

Beside me, Wilf was hit in the body and leg by small arms fire, and lay slumped on the grilles, his chest heaving. I put my body over the woman as the Tiger swayed back again, reversing up the ramp and onto the bridge span itself.

I glimpsed, around the turret, our own precious Tiger.

Its front hull was shot away and its engine deck was burning fully, with parts of the turret hanging off. A superb machine, a slayer and protector of men, smashed to pieces under the Red hammer. Beside it, one of the bunkers had its entire roof blown away by an SU shell, and the concrete slab crashed down onto the few troops who were trying to escape through its rear doors, crushing them under tonnes of mass. The remaining mortar troops abandoned their weapons and bolted for the bridge. I saw the body of the grey-haired artillery officer lying on the river bank. Had he set his timing device to blow the bridge?

The other bunker was being assaulted by a Stalin tank which was driving along its wall, under the slit embrasure, with a Red soldier standing on the turret roof, caring nothing for his life. He was armed with a flamethrower, and he was pouring a stream of fire through the embrasure, flooding the inside with orange flames.

The PAK gun was submerged in fire which overflowed the aperture and gushed down the walls. The flame-gunner was shot down by the last MG post in the bunker wall, sending him tumbling into the snow to burn among his own flames – but his task was done. As we reversed away over the bridge, both bunkers erupted in orange fire.

We clung to the Tiger's hull, choking on its acrid fumes, while it reversed over the wreckage on the bridge, crushing bodies and smaller vehicles as it retreated. A Stalin tank lumbered up onto the ramp, but the manoeuvre exposed its underside for a moment, and the Tiger gunner fired a round directly into its belly. The Red tank shook and rolled back, trailing smoke.

The Tiger's rear turret hatch opened, and the gunner looked out at us.

'That was our last round, Herr Ober.'

'Good man. The bridge will blow soon. Very soon.'

At the entry to the bridge, between the blazing fortifications, the few remnants of our German infantry began a frantic scramble to get across. It was better for them to die in this attempt than to be caught by the Russians on the other side, as the JS tanks and their ground troops began to swarm between the bunkers. A dozen Germans ran at full tilt, some throwing aside their weapons, swerving between pursuing fire, vaulting the corpses and debris in their path. Of the dozen troops, I think that three or four made it across, chasing after us as our Tiger thumped down onto the German-held side, skidding backwards in the frozen snow.

As we came to a halt, up against a blockhouse, Helmann and I jumped off, dragging the Russian woman with us. We threw ourselves with her behind a sandbagged wall, the object of much interest to the handful Panzergrenadiers who were in position there already with an MG42.

'Now the bridge will blow,' Helmann said. 'Now!'

On the abandoned bank, the Reds were engaged in a frenzy of destruction, the SU guns firing again and again into the ruined forts, and the infantry machine-gunning into the slit trenches which must already be full of corpses.

From that maelstrom, another Stalin tank moved up onto the bridge, straddling the width with its broad tracks, and came lurching towards us, eager to be the first onto the German side, whatever the cost. It fired on us, but we were low down on the German ramp, and the shell screamed over our heads in a streak of orange. The Stalin began firing wildly as it advanced, shooting into the German territory – and, looking around, I saw that there were plenty of targets here. There was a unit of Panthers, only just arriving and still moving into position; several Tigers, still in their narrow transportation tracks, meaning that they had come straight from the railhead. Behind them, more armour was moving up: a column of Stugs, and a few of the big Marder self-propelled guns, surely enough to hold back these Stalins and infantry for good.

'The bridge must blow now,' Helmann said, as if giving it a direct order.

Nothing happened.

On the bridge, though, that Stalin was getting closer, crushing the already mangled corpses and debris on the surface, and smashing against the upright girders as it accelerated across. Behind it, a second Stalin was emerging onto the bridge – and beyond that, I got a glimpse of other Stalins and an SU, actively jostling each other for the status of being among the first to storm the crossing point.

Our Tiger had no ammunition remaining, but the other German armour on this side of the river belatedly sprang to action, beginning to fire on the Russian vehicles in a storm of red and white tracer. That first Stalin was reaching the end of the bridge now, though, and was almost on top of us; it was traversing and firing at whatever it could see, as our shells slammed into its armour. Behind it, there were another two Stalins moving on the bridge by now, clearly intent on bursting across and leading a spearhead into our lands.

'The bridge,' Helmann shouted into the air. 'Blow the bridge.'

As the leading Stalin thumped down onto the ramp right in front of us, the bridge finally blew. The noise was colossal – louder than anything else I had heard in the war, and for a few seconds everything and everyone froze still, except for the disintegrating bridge.

The aircraft bombs built into its supports detonated one by one, within a fraction of a second of each other, in a wave of explosions which roared back from our bank to the Russian bank. The steel uprights rose into the air and span sideways, while the wooden surface was driven into thousands of fragments, whirling distantly into the river and across the land.

Caught in the rolling blast, the two audacious Stalins on the bridge were thrown sideways, their running gear shearing off and flying into the water as they span over and crashed into the river upside down. The very last of the demolition bombs caught an SU gun as it tried to reverse back off the ramp, and blew its gun and mantle completely off its hull, sending the huge gun tumbling end-over-end against the walls of the burning bunker.

Debris showered down on us, on our reinforcements, falling all along the river bank and for a great distance along the river. All that remained of the crossing were a few girder beams projecting jaggedly from the churning water, where the two Stalins had disappeared under the surface.

With my ears ringing, I tried to take in the changed situation.

The single Stalin that had reached our side stood stationary on our ramp, with its engine running and its turret rotating, perhaps still taking stock of the number of enemies now ranged against it. Our Panthers, our Tigers, all our fresh and fully-loaded armour, even the big Marder guns, all traversed and focussed on this one solitary Russian invader.

Bravely, the Red commander chose to advance, not to reverse into the river. The Stalin lurched forward, flames shooting from its exhausts, and smashed past the Tiger that had carried us over the bridge, knocking it aside. The Stalin had time to fire one shot, which flew out uselessly across our territory into the distance, before our guns opened fire.

The Stalin was shot to pieces in moments. Rounds pierced the turret and blew fragments away, while its tracks were ripped off and sent whipping through the air, scattering broken links into the river. Its momentum carried it some distance along the road away from the bridge, trailing a sheet of flames; but when it ground to a halt it was knocked left and right by the blows that rained down on it. The upper hull lifted up, revealing a furnace inside, full of burning fuel and exploding ammunition. Then even the hull roof was ripped away, leaving the turret to collapse down into the flames.

—

We went to the Tiger to check on Wilf, who was still lying on the engine deck. He was dead, with his face turned towards the western horizon, where the Reich began.

Helmann shook his head, holding the Russian woman with her arms pinned behind her back. Then he flagged down an armoured car among the reinforcement forces, and explained his mission to the crew. They took us on board, and in the cramped compartment, they drove us at speed away from the river, away from the crossing point that had cost so much blood to defend, along roads crowded with troops and vehicles, to the nearest Divisional headquarters.

'We have been successful,' Helmann yelled to me, over the roar of the armoured car's engine and the clatter of other vehicles on the road. 'The crossing point has been defended. Our border zone is secured. This has been a great day for us, Faust. A magnificent day.'

'Sir.'

'To complete our success now, we will hand our prisoner personally to the intelligence team. And those gentlemen at the interrogation centre will make this Red bitch talk, believe me. They know how to get a pretty tongue wagging.'

The Russian woman, understanding his German words, stared at him through bloodshot, terrified eyes.

—

The sun had passed its zenith, and was growing bigger in front of us, lighting up the western plateau with swathes of a smoky, crimson light. The armoured car took some time to reach the command point in the rear. We had to make our way through columns of armoured infantry in Hanomags streaming down to the river zone; these men were fresh, well-fed and in white-camouflaged winter suits. Beside them, lines of Panzer IVs and Panthers waited to advance, their surfaces neatly whitewashed to blend with the snow. It was a real battlegroup, and I was confident that this force could hold that narrow river crossing against the Ivans indefinitely if needed.

The conflict would surely be grim, though.

I looked out of the car's open turret at the eastern horizon, where the crossing point lay. It was lit up again and again with red and white flashes, and columns of smoke rose enormous distances into the air. Overhead, I saw three Messerschmitt fighters race to the east, their wings trailing vapour in the leaden sky. At one point, a group of Sturmoviks appeared over the fields to the north, carpet bombing the land in bursts of orange fire. They turned and banked away, with no Flak being fired, and no Luftwaffe in the sky at all.

'*Scheisse*,' the commander of the armoured car said to me, watching the smoke rise from the fields. 'That was our Tiger regiment.'

I said nothing, and I noticed that the road was now less choked with transports, as if everything we had in reserve had already been sent to the line.

When we pulled up at the command point, Hellmann accepted the salutes of the armoured car crew, and gestured me to bring the woman into the building. I held her by the arm, and found that she was trembling as we went inside. The command point was a wooden forestry cabin of two storeys, reinforced with sandbags and earth mounds. It stretched back a long way, with many sub-rooms visible off a long central corridor lit by a kerosene lamp. Staff teams were hurrying around, carrying papers and calling out updates on the movement of the reinforcements.

While Helmann went to brief the intelligence officers about the prisoner, I stood guard over the woman in a side room piled with stores. There were Russian religious icons on the walls, and the woman crossed herself piously when she saw them.

She stood opposite me, and I held Hellmann's MP40 cradled in one arm.

It was suddenly quiet. After all the noise, all the charging, this was a strange sensation, and the amphetamines were declining in my bloodstream, making me feel exhausted.

'What will they do to me here?' she asked me in German.

'I don't know,' I replied – although in fact I had a very good idea of the methods they would employ on her. 'How is it that you speak German?'

Her eyes filled with tears.

'I studied German literature at University. I know nothing of any important military matters,' she said, wiping her nose.

I watched her face.

'Then why did the Russians come looking to find you, in those tanks? Why did they try to rescue you?'

'Listen to me, and I'll tell you. This is the truth. I am the mistress of a senior Russian officer. He is very senior, and I am his woman. One of his women. This is his Army, and he can do what he wishes. I think that he wants to get me back.'

Overhead, aircraft flew low, and a Flak spat from somewhere close. There were explosions, and the building shook. In the corridor, men were shouting, demanding information. Then it quietened down.

'That doesn't sound true at all,' I said. 'Why would a Russian General have his mistress in uniform, in a bunker in the front line?'

'I accompany him in the line. He takes me with him everywhere. I have the uniform of a radio operator, but in fact I am purely his mistress. He was inspecting the bunkers when you advanced on them. When you attacked, I was left behind in all the chaos.'

'He just left you behind?'

'Yes.'

I stood watching her. The icons on the wall glowed a fiery red colour in the declining sun. Her red hair was loose and grimy.

'Please,' she whispered. 'You are a good man.'

'I am not a good man.'

'You are. You saved me from the fire in the tank.'

'Because my officer told me to.'

'You would have saved me anyway.'

'No.'

'Yes, I believe that you would have.'

There was the sound of explosions in the distance, which made her jump.

'Please,' she said. 'They will torture me here. They will hurt me in a terrible way. I have no information to give them, and that will make it worse. They will kill me in the end, but it might take days for me to die.'

I looked into her eyes. She was shaking, but her pupils were dilated with energy, with some kind of hope.

'And all this was for no purpose,' she said, in a whisper. 'All of this was for nothing. Everything you have done, and everything I have done, it is all for nothing. I ask you now, please let something good come from this. Something.'

I lit a cigarette, and gave it to her. She smoked it with trembling hands, but she didn't look me in the eyes again, ever. She had said what she could say, and now I had to decide.

Was it true, that all of this was for nothing? The shooting, the burning, the crushed bodies? My father, mother and sister, lost forever under the mountain of rubble in Munich? Big, ugly Kurt, and Wilf, and the pilots and the gunners, all the drivers and loaders and soldiers. How could so much be done, and all of it for nothing?

It was impossible that this could be for nothing, I decided. Impossible.

There was a door into an orchard outside the cabin, where frozen trees stood grey against the sky. I opened the door and told her to stand outside, among the trees.

She nodded, and touched my face, still without looking at me.

She went outside. She stood with her face against the first tree, and I shot her with the MP40. Two shots in the back of the head, so easy to fire. Her head blew open, and her body slumped among the roots of the trees in the snow. That was her death, and that would be her grave.

A few seconds passed, while I got my story straight in my mind.

Then Helmann burst into the room, followed by an officer in the insignia of the intelligence branch.

'What was that shooting?' Helmann demanded. 'And where is my prisoner, Faust, damn you?'

'She tried to escape, Herr Ober.'

'What in God's name do you mean?'

'She said there are partisans in the woods around this post, sir, and she said they will rescue her and return her to the Russian lines. She said she had gathered information about our forces in this zone, and memorised our positions. Then she ran into the orchard to escape. For that reason, Herr Ober, I shot her.'

Helmann cursed me. He punched me on the chest with his gloved hand, called me a *verdamm* useless fool, and he seized the MP40 from me. The intelligence officer went and examined the body, which was surrounded by a halo of red in the snow. The intelligence man came back and studied me in silence for several seconds, while my throat went dry. I tried not to swallow or blink.

Then he relaxed and shrugged.

'It is certainly a lost opportunity, gentlemen, and most regrettable. I would have enjoyed the chance to interrogate that particular prisoner. But such things happen. And we must leave here now, anyway. This sector is no longer secure.' He looked outside again. 'There may well be partisans around.'

—

In the road outside, I stood with Helmann as the Divisional staff burned documents on a fire, and loaded others into cars and trucks. All the vehicles were pointing to the west.

'The sector is no longer secure, Herr Ober?' I asked. 'What does that mean?'

'The Reds have bridged the river at the crossing point,' Helmann said, in a factual way, entirely without emotion.

'They've crossed the river?' I said. 'But the bridge was destroyed. We saw it.'

Helmann laughed in his *unheimlich* manner.

'After we left, the Red planes bombed our armour on the western bank. We had no Flak, and the Luftwaffe was nowhere in sight, apparently. Then the Reds used Katyushas for an hour to burn the pieces. All of our panzers, the guns, they were all bombed and burned. Now the Reds have used pontoon boats to put a bridge across the river right there, over the old bridge. They have armour building up on our side now, and they're breaking through. They're coming west across the plateau even now.' He laughed again. 'This Russian General must be a real swine. He drives his men to death, and they simply ask for more.'

He shouldered his MP40. I noticed that he had somehow taken the opportunity to polish his boots, which were as glossy as ever before.

'Now I will form our unit again,' he said, 'with new panzers, and new men. There is another river, twenty kilometres to the west, and it's much more heavily fortified than the last one. We can certainly hold the Reds there. There is no doubt this time. We will make a fine name for ourselves there, I can assure you.'

'Yes, Herr Ober.'

'But damn you to hell, Faust. I thought you were smart, but you're a fool after all. If you'd guarded that prisoner properly, at least some good would have come out of this wretched situation. You saved her from the fire in the panzer, and you protected her, and it was all for no result at all.' Helmann reached for his hip flask. 'All for no *verdamm* result at all.' He wiped his mouth and handed me the cognac. 'But it's done, and we are busy. I shall say no more about it for now. Let's find ourselves a car, and get moving. *Panzer Marsch!*'

—

*The publisher wishes to highlight that the text of this book contains opinions which originated in the German experience of the Second World War. These opinions are not shared by the current publisher, and the publisher does not condone or promote such views. They are presented in the interests of historical understanding only.*

—

By the same author:

**Wolfgang Faust's astonishing account of his breakout from the Halbe Kessel in April 1945, entitled 'The Last Panther.'**

'The Last Panther' is a ruthless description of the German 9th Army's attempts to escape Russian encirclement against all odds in the last weeks of the war. It is a phenomenal memoir of panzer warfare, the collapse of the Third Reich and the appalling suffering of civilians and troops on all sides, as World War 2 drew to an apocalyptic conclusion in the fields of Germany.

The latest WW2 reading from Sprech Media…

**Personal accounts of June 6th 1944 by Wehrmacht soldiers who experienced the Normandy beach landings.**

Most accounts of D Day are told from the Allied perspective, with its emphasis on how the German resistance was overcome on June 6th 1944. But what was it like to be a German soldier in the bunkers, the trenches and gun emplacements of the Normandy coast, facing the onslaught of the mightiest seaborne invasion in history? What motivated the German defenders, and how did they fight among the dunes and fields on that first cataclysmic day?

This book sheds fascinating light on these questions, bringing together statements made by German survivors after the war, when time had allowed them to reflect on their state of mind, their actions and choices of June 6th. We see a perspective of D Day which deserves to be added to the historical record, in which ordinary German troops struggled to make sense of the onslaught that was facing them, and emerged stunned at the resources and sheer determination of the Allied soldiers.

Made in the USA
Columbia, SC
06 December 2019